Mind of a Survivor

Mind of a Survivor

*What the wild has taught me
about survival and success*

MEGAN HINE

CORONET

First published in Great Britain in 2017 by Coronet
An imprint of Hodder & Stoughton
An Hachette UK company

1

A CIP catalogue record for this title is available from the British Library

Hardback ISBN: 978 1 473 64928 6
Trade Paperback ISBN: 978 1 473 64929 3
Ebook ISBN: 978 1 473 64930 9

Typeset in Bembo by Palimpsest Book Production Limited,
Falkirk, Stirlingshire

Printed and bound by Clays Ltd, St Ives plc

Hodder & Stoughton policy is to use papers that are natural, renewable
and recyclable products and made from wood grown in sustainable
forests. The logging and manufacturing processes are expected to conform to
the environmental regulations of the country of origin.

Hodder & Stoughton Ltd
Carmelite House
50 Victoria Embankment
London EC4Y 0DZ

www.hodder.co.uk

I would like to dedicate this book to Nana. Thank you for teaching me the values of being insightful and non-judgemental and to always be open minded and explore the world. You are an incredible role model.

I would also like to dedicate this book to anyone questioning their inner strength. I very much hope you find a ray of light somewhere in this book. You are stronger than you believe right now.

Contents

Introduction

There's a popular Rule of Three you'll hear if you ever go on a survival course: three minutes without air, three days without water, three weeks without food. I'd like to add another: three seconds without thinking, because nothing will kill you quicker in the wilderness than switching off and making a bad decision.

I've led hundreds of expeditions through just about every terrain on earth and worked behind the scenes on many of TV's most popular survival shows. I've seen people become paralysed by fear and sabotage themselves through self-doubt, but I've also seen heroes emerge, people who find their voice and their way when life pushes them to the absolute limit. Why is that? Why do some people have the mind of a survivor when others do not? In this book, I'm going to explore this question by sharing some of my wildest adventures. I'm also going to show how what we do in our everyday lives can mentally prepare us for a crisis.

Disaster usually strikes without warning, whether it's a terrorist incident in a city centre, a plane crash in a jungle or an earthquake in an idyllic landscape. If something goes disastrously wrong in a remote place, the sobering fact is that very few of us will make it back to civilisation. Having a bit of training and carrying the right gear can make a difference, but the single thing that marks people out for survival is their attitude. Those who find inner strength, who remain determined in the face of adversity and are alert to possibility are the ones who do the best. And that means we all have the power to be survivors, not just the young and the fit.

The past few years have seen a massive surge in interest in adventure lifestyles, and I've read lots of survival stories that focus on the physical aspect of the survivor's ordeal. How low did the overnight temperatures fall? How long were they submerged? How much pain were they in? These stories rarely discuss how people handled their fears and emotions. It was the same when I was little, reading about explorers like Ernest Shackleton and Scott of the Antarctic: the focus was always on starvation or injuries or frostbite, and I remember thinking, Yes, but how did they cope? What was going through their heads?

I'm fairly sure I understand why these emotions are missing from survival stories: from my own experience I know that one of the ways we endure extreme hardships is by shutting down our emotional responses. If you let fear, pain, distress and anxiety rise to the surface they can paralyse your mind and stop it functioning. When you add in the macho stigma of talking about emotions, and a tradition for maintaining a stiff upper lip, it is easy to see why adventurers leave this stuff off the page when they write their memoirs.

And yet it's been my experience that the mental side of survival is more important than fitness and experience. My guess is it doesn't get the attention it deserves for the same reasons physical health is still prioritised over mental health: we're not comfortable talking about it. Thankfully, this is starting to change, but it's only in the fairly recent past in Western medicine we've begun treating people rather than diseases – taking a holistic approach to health – because we've found that a purely scientific attitude to well-being won't cure some illnesses: we also need to soothe our minds.

Along with the rise of the adventure industry, there has been an increased interest in traditional bushcraft skills, like fire-making, foraging, hunting and building shelters. It's striking how many people get so much out of learning these ancient crafts, but it's not at all surprising. When I work with native peoples who still practise their ancestral skills and heritage, I never cease to be inspired and amazed by the similarities between skills used on opposite sides of the globe, as well as the quirks and adaptations different tribes have added so they can work with, or conquer, their environment. Who wouldn't be awestruck, as I was, by a tribe that lives alongside horses, and who – when dehydrated or in need of energy on long, barren rides – let blood from their ponies and drink just enough from a vein to give them an energy boost? These insights make us realise how much we've lost in the modern world, but they're also clues as to how – if we're alert, open and inquisitive – we can thrive in any environment.

Bushcraft and traditional skills reconnect us with something primal, and spending time in the wilderness and discovering lost arts have huge therapeutic benefits. For a day or two, people on my courses become part of a temporary community and they leave feeling more connected to the world. They often tell me they've learnt something they can use in an emergency – but bushcraft skills are more about making yourself comfortable *after* you've survived. They are traditional living skills and a lot of them take time to perform – which is a big part of their contemporary appeal – but time is the one thing you rarely have when disaster hits.

Bushcraft skills are part of the toolkit I take into the wild, along with my experience, but what fascinates me are the people who survive without having any of my skills or experience. People who have been in plane crashes or shipwrecks, people who were completely unprepared and not especially fit, yet still make it home. What makes a survivor? Why *do* some people survive while others don't? I think it has to be because survival is less to do with fire-making and spear-fishing and much more to do with being creative, inventive, open-minded, and having the ability to make good decisions under pressure.

4

In the wild that pressure is immense. If you think of times when you've experienced pressure in your own life – maybe giving a talk at work or sitting an exam – and were unable to find the words to express yourself or perform at your best, just imagine what the stresses of a survival situation would do to your ability to think clearly. You're cold, thirsty, hungry, exhausted, covered with insect bites and blisters . . . and you're hanging from the edge of a cliff with one hand. Even people who are very used to making decisions in their day-to-day lives struggle when they're truly tested by the wilderness.

Often, it's the people you least expect who truly thrive. The overtly macho guys who fit the survivalist stereotype may be covering holes in their resilience by being loud and outspoken. Once you take them out of their comfort zone and force them to come face to face with demons they don't know how to handle, they crumble. On the flipside, I've seen stay-at-home mothers, who initially come across as timid, find an inner strength and resourcefulness that surprises everyone, including themselves.

I truly believe that everyone has the capacity to overcome extreme hardship and to be resilient enough to make it home. That durability comes more easily to some, so I want to show how, through my own experiences and observations, anyone can build up their resilience and increase their chances of becoming a survivor. That's not to say survival skills and general fitness don't have immense value – they buy you valuable time – but they don't stop you making stupid decisions or guarantee you'll find the inner strength and fighting spirit to keep you going.

It's been my experience that people who empathise with their environment and who respond instinctively to others make better survivors, and that often means women. In some of the tribal communities I've visited, women are usually taking care of children, preparing meals, setting traps and looking for roots while the men – more often than not – are doing the big-game hunting. Because the women carry out so many tasks, they are more adaptable, and being able to deal with several things at once is a key survival characteristic. Survival isn't about single-minded determination, it's about seeing the whole picture, and that includes knowing yourself.

Youth is often thought to be another signifier of doing well in the wild. I suspect that has as much to do with young people's curiosity about the world as it does with their relative fitness: how you think in the wild plays just as big a part in survival as what you do. How you view the wilderness – as something to explore and understand rather than as an impenetrable barrier – will help you survive.

My interest in the psychology of survival ignited when I studied for a degree in Outdoor Education. I took a module on Eastern European Philosophies of Outdoor Education that explored what drives people to go into the wild. I also completed one called 'A Personal Response to a Mountain Environment', which turned out to be life-changing.

It required students to spend seven days alone in the Picos de Europa Mountains in northern Spain. The idea was that we were to immerse ourselves in the environment and keep a diary to help us examine our interactions with, and responses to, the landscape. We were all in the same area, but were far enough apart not to see each other for the entire week.

The Picos de Europa range is wild – there are still lynxes, Europe's leopard-like big cats, living up in those mountains – and it can be as harsh as it is beautiful. All I packed was a sleeping-bag, a bivvy bag, a knife, a pen and a notebook. Some of the other students headed off into the mountains with tents and food, but I planned to make my own shelter and find my food.

It was late spring and, as I walked up, I could see the beautiful rocky valley start to come into life, but almost the moment I got up to altitude it started to snow. And it didn't stop snowing for the entire seven days. Without a tent, I needed to find shelter and came across a massive boulder with a shelf underneath that was protected from the snow. I got inside, built a little wall around it, using rocks that were lying about, and made it my home for the next week. I quickly realised two things: it was so barren up there that there was nothing to eat (except the meagre snack of a mouse, whose home I had seemingly moved into), and there was also nothing to burn.

With hindsight, the remarkable thing is that I don't really remember being cold or hungry. I look at that week now as a real coming-of-age experience, not unlike the tribal rituals that send adolescents off into the wilderness to find their spirit animal and get to know themselves. Once I'd discovered there was no firewood and nothing to eat I decided to see what happened. Obviously, eventually, I would have died without food, but I knew that for a week it wasn't going to kill me. So I just stepped out of reality and entered a different place.

I was nineteen at the time, and being alone without food turned out to be incredibly interesting. I began to think about why I interacted with stimulae in certain ways and how I processed the experiences. I was getting in tune with the mountains, but I was also tuning into myself. When I read my notes from that week now, it was clear I was having an almost out-of-body experience. It was very spiritual, which was completely unexpected because I had always been a very practical person, and spirituality had not been a big factor in my upbringing.

During the day, I'd go off exploring. I didn't have a watch. I had no idea what time it was – and I didn't know how to use the sun to tell the time back then – so I was just going with my natural body rhythms, and relying on my instincts. I became hyperaware of the ways in which my mind and body were connected. I entered a childlike state, which was all about exploration and playing in the environment. It wasn't a conscious decision to enter this state: I just stepped into it.

I became fascinated with everything, from the way the clouds moved across the sky to the daily habits of the little mouse I shared the boulder with. I had this incredible sense of wonder about everything I was seeing and feeling. It was one of the most profound and remarkable experiences of my life, and I came away with a much greater awareness of who I was and how I fitted into the world. I also learnt that there's no room for ego in the wild. It doesn't care about your insecurities, it doesn't owe you anything: the wild is neutral.

Without anything to read, or watch, or anyone to talk to, I experienced a solitude in which I discovered there is an energy that flows through everything. If your mind is open, I found, that energy can flow through you too. It was – and still is – the most incredible feeling, but when the sun came up on the final morning I knew it was time to trek down and meet up with my tutor and the other students.

When I got there I was stunned to find that, of fifteen students, only three of us had stayed out for the entire seven days. I wanted to understand why I hadn't just toughed it out but had had the experience of a lifetime when most of the others had given up. That was when I started considering the role psychology plays in our survival.

You might expect that the people with shelter and food would have fared better than me, but that clearly hadn't been the case. Perhaps my lack of a tent, which meant there had been nothing between me and the landscape, had helped. The people under canvas, by contrast, had zipped themselves in when the weather got bad and become detached from their surroundings. Without the stimulation, they hadn't developed the sense of wonder that had so inspired me. I think they just got bored.

I also wonder if I thrived because I went into that week without any expectations. Mostly we approach a new situation – whether social or work-related – with a sense of how we should behave, what we hope to get out of it or our definition of success. If we don't achieve our goals we feel frustration and anger, emotions that are hard to deal with when you're on your own for days on end. Perhaps the others had envisaged how their week would be, and when the reality didn't compare, they felt let down in some way.

No matter where I work, or whom I work with, I'm constantly reminded of the role psychology plays in our survival. I've been particularly interested in the findings of Dr Al Siebert, who spent forty years studying resilience. He didn't just work with wilderness survivors, he studied a wide range of people, from patients who had been treated for cancer to women who had endured years of domestic abuse and to soldiers who had seen combat.

Some of Siebert's patients came to his clinic because they feared they were bi-polar, or had schizophrenia, and they wanted to understand why they seemed to be at both ends of the spectrum. He noticed that many had endured life experiences that would make most of us seek therapy, but that wasn't why they had turned to him for help. They had coped with the trauma: they simply wanted to understand the extremes of their personality. Siebert concluded that resilient people have very complex personalities and are capable of experiencing conflicting emotions. He realised that what makes somebody resilient, enabling them to cope with whatever life throws at them, is the ability to feel lots of different emotions, often conflicting ones, sometimes simultaneously. People with more defined personalities, he noted, struggled in complex and difficult environments. Of course, there's nothing more complex and difficult than a survival situation, whether it's domestic abuse, active war or a natural disaster: survival takes many forms.

One of Siebert's more interesting findings was that, in daily life, natural survivors tend to be invisible, the kind of people who blend into the background. They're often not in leadership positions and don't have alpha personalities. The people around them might consider them lazy because if things are going well they don't waste energy shouting about how great they are. When things go wrong, though, they step forwards and take control. They have spent so long observing their environment that they seem to have an expanded awareness of what is required. When I read Siebert's work, I immediately heard echoes of my experience in the Picos de Europa.

Siebert also found that dealing with one kind of trauma made people better able to handle another: exposure to testing environments makes you more likely to cope in other situations. Since discovering this, I've led hundreds of expeditions and it's not uncommon for clients to book themselves onto an adventure after a life-altering event, like illness, divorce or bereavement. More often than not, they respond better than others to the challenges of the wild.

Siebert's work has helped me imagine resilience to be

like the immune system: when your body is exposed to a new virus or bacteria, your immune system has to learn how to defeat the invasion, which is why you feel pretty rough. The next time you're exposed to the same contagion, your body knows how to fight and initiates a much more effective response. The same happens with emotional trauma: at first it can be overwhelming, but the next time you experience distress, you'll have learnt how to deal with it a bit better.

I have tried to scrutinise my own behaviour and work out not just what I can change that will be more likely to lead to my survival, but also why I keep following a career that puts it in jeopardy. It is hard to step back from something that is second nature to me and analyse myself, but I've realised I do the work I do because I'm driven to it. If I sit still for too long, panic drives me back outdoors. I'm incredibly tough on myself, and the wild is the place where I can keep pushing and testing my boundaries, without endangering anyone else. What I do may be risky, but for me it's healthy.

The expeditions I've been on have helped me conclude that a handful of characteristics, when combined, produce the best survivors. We all possess them, but while some of us use them naturally, others don't tap into them at all. What I hope to show in this book is that we don't have to wait for a survival situation to practise these skills: we can all develop a survivor mindset as we go about our daily lives. These characteristics – or abilities – are intuition, creativity, empathy, adaptability and flexibility. They might not be what you'll read about in other adventure books (they're not as gung-ho or physical as most people expect from a survival expert) but I believe that if you can access them you've got the ability to survive and thrive, not just in the wilderness but in your career and personal life too.

1

The Developing Mind

I'm a little unusual in my line of work because I haven't been in the military. Many of my colleagues learnt their skills in uniform and naturally gravitated towards adventurous careers after they left their regiments. My path was a little different, and a little less planned. I never had any idea what I would do when I left school: I just knew I had an overwhelming urge to be outdoors.

I'm the eldest of four children and was the trailblazer for my parents, leading them through the previously unexplored lands of parenthood. I grew up on the Malvern Hills and was encouraged to get involved in things like ballet (which I loved *and* hated *and* was crap at) and music. I played the violin (well enough to join the Children's English Symphony

Orchestra), but I was also encouraged to get outside, and often returned home dirty and dishevelled after a day with my siblings in the hills. My parents fuelled my passion for the outdoors by taking us on caravanning and walking holidays in the UK's wildernesses. Looking back now, I see these were the first steps on the path that led to where I am now.

The next step was mountain-biking, which I discovered by chance on my way home from school when I was about thirteen. I was riding my father's old bike with a basket on the back when I wondered if, instead of taking the road, I could ride along the hills behind our house. I still remember the first big descent I did, totally out of control with dodgy brakes, skidding on loose gravel. The basket fell off with the vibrations, but as I dragged it home I had a huge grin on my face. It was the start of a new era of freedom as I discovered the exhilaration of pushing myself just to see how far I could ride, or what I could ride up . . . or how fast I could make the descent. I had no idea about training or the importance of taking rest days, so when I felt tired I took it as a sign to push myself harder or go further. I know now this is against all training principles, but I think it gave me the physical foundation to endure pain and hardship.

I had a restless, wandering nature and felt most alive and fulfilled out in the mountains. As I got older I spent as much time as I could, often on my own, climbing and mountain-biking, testing myself and pushing against every boundary I came up against. I found being indoors, especially classrooms, restrictive; I still find it nearly impossible to sit still for long inside.

Until my early teens I ran around with the boys as one of them: I didn't see the difference between me and them. I always had scraped knees or holes in my tights and was often told off for play-fighting. In many ways, boys were easier to understand: if they had a problem they'd fight it out and it'd be over. With girls it tended to be mental warfare, and I didn't have the patience for manipulative games. Looking back, I was probably a bit feral and out of control.

I really wasn't interested in clothes but I do remember in my early teens suddenly hating all my torn, patched, hand-me-down outfits when I noticed other girls wore much nicer things. It was a horrible moment of self-awareness and, for the next year or so, I became very self-conscious. Now I know that it's something everyone goes through as their body changes, but at the time I found the release I needed in mountain-biking: it was where I felt most myself and it didn't matter what I wore or what anyone thought of me.

Through my school, I got the chance to join the military cadets and was taken on climbing, kayaking, mountaineering and camping expeditions all over the UK. Although I was always the only girl, I experienced a profound sense of belonging and thought that maybe I'd go into the military after school. My parents had to give special permission for me to go on those trips as there weren't any female super-visors, and I'm so grateful now that they did; also that the military personnel who ran the organisation saw my love of adventure and found a way for me to participate.

My parents were always supportive, but I think they assumed I'd eventually go down the academic route and head for university, which they had worked hard to achieve for themselves. I left school with A levels in biology, chemistry, geography and art. At one point I thought about studying marine biology at university, but I knew that being stuck inside, whether in lectures or in an office, was not a future I wanted. And I couldn't see an obvious career path that would involve me in the things I was passionate about. I decided I needed to see more of the world, so I took a giant leap and went on a gap year.

I had dreamt of going to New Zealand since I was eight when I'd been given a book called *The Land of the Long White Cloud*. It was filled with stunning images and Maori mythology and completely captured my imagination. After my A levels, I saved enough money for a ticket and got a placement, via a gap-year organisation, at a school near Christchurch where I photocopied and made tea. Not the adventure I had gone looking for! I lasted two weeks before I bought my first car, for two hundred New Zealand dollars, and went exploring.

By chance, I ran into a couple of guys who had just started an apprenticeship in a remote outdoor centre in the middle of the South Island. It turned out the centre was looking for another apprentice. I jumped at the chance to join them and spent the rest of my gap year training as a raft guide, taking school groups on long-distance hikes and teaching rock-climbing. In my spare time, I went exploring on my own. Needless to say, I didn't want to come back to the UK, but when I found out about a degree course in Outdoor Studies, I realised it might just be possible to make a career out of being in the wild.

At university in the Lake District I found people who had my restless spirit, who shared my need for the outdoors and were also driven by their passions. Finally it was normal to get up at 3 a.m. to go ice-climbing before a 9 a.m. lecture (and then go drinking until midnight before you did it all over again the following day). Like most students, I paid my way by getting a part-time job: I qualified as a mountain leader and, instead of working in a bar or clearing tables, I took clients on expeditions, gaining valuable work experience in the process.

Just before graduation, I had an experience that guided me a little further along my eventual career path. I was alone at the top of Bowfell Buttress in the Lake District, watching sheep chase each other. A thought popped into my head: everything I had with me was to protect myself from nature. The waterproof clothing, the bivvy, the stove . . . it was all about keeping me separate from the elements. I wasn't working with the environment, I was battling against it. For someone who called themselves an outdoor enthusiast, there seemed something a bit twisted about that. It was a real moment of revelation.

Then, just a few days later, a friend had a spare ticket for a bushcraft talk run by a local company. I had no idea what bushcraft was, but I wasn't doing anything so I went with him. Needless to say, I was blown away by the lecture, which was all about working with the environment rather than taming it. It was exactly what I felt had been missing. The guy giving the talk had worked with native peoples who used trees and plants for medicinal and even spiritual purposes, and I grasped how little I understood of the wilderness I loved. After the talk I went to the company's website and saw they were looking for people to work with them.

I sent them my CV, thinking there was no way they'd give me a job, but when I graduated I started a two-year apprenticeship with them. It opened up a whole new world, and taught me about the different properties of certain trees and the medicinal uses of plants. It was hard work, but it was also amazing. In the winter I paid my bills by working as an off-road driving instructor, but in the summer I lived out in the hills in a shelter I'd built, getting up super-early to do my camp chores so I could then sit in on the instructors' lectures. They were like walking encyclopedias, and I wanted not just to have their knowledge but to use it too.

That led to other work in the adventure and travel industry, and I started leading groups in the Himalayas and the Alps. In 2007, while I was running the outdoor programme at an international school in Switzerland, I was approached to work with Bear Grylls on his hugely successful *Man vs Wild* show where he battles alone through remote places to make it back to civilisation. I had the fortunate – and slightly random – combination of rope skills, guiding skills and bushcraft knowledge, which the producers needed.

Bear and his team made me really welcome. I was instantly impressed by his ability to talk to camera while performing amazing stunts, and I developed a deep respect for him. He doesn't just stick up for what he believes but also for his team while inspiring the people around him.

I was invited back to work on more episodes of *Man vs Wild*, and through the contacts I made I was asked to work on other shows. These days, I often scout filming locations, looking for places that are remote and spectacular, but that are also accessible for a film crew. During filming, I might rig up challenges for the onscreen talent, like abseiling or zip-wire stunts.

There are usually two core safety crew members who oversee TV shows, and we'll hire local guides and specialists as required. Depending on the terrain, the safety crew can be as big as the production team – which creates its own challenges when access is tight and locations are remote: we need one safety expert for every camera operator and sound technician. On steep terrain, for example, we'll short-rope the camera and sound operators so they can get the footage they need while we concentrate on their safety. Camera operators in particular are so focused on filming the action they can't always see their feet so we act as their eyes, hold them steady . . . and absorb their falls, should they slip. I also get asked to work as a survival consultant, which can involve advising a production team on what can be eaten, how to trap an animal or build a shelter.

It was while working on a shoot in the Arctic that I first met a guy called Stani who, after we'd spent a few years working together, became my partner in love and life. We continue to work together on some projects, and through a combination of TV assignments and expedition-leading, we spend eleven months of the year away from home, in every kind of terrain from the equator to the poles. Sometimes we work together in intense, high pressure situations, and sometimes we spend months apart on different continents.

Nothing about my career has been planned, including ending up in front of the camera. I had taken a job guiding a team of contestants on a Swiss TV show, and it was only when we started filming that I was told I'd be on screen. My initial reaction was 'This is not what I signed up for', but it was too late to back out so I gave it a go. I didn't expect to enjoy it, but I quickly discovered it was another way of sharing my passion for the wild.

My TV work means journalists want to interview me, and at first I was surprised to be asked about my experience as a woman in the survival industry. I'm so used to being the only woman in the room (or the tent, or the cave) that I'd never seen it as unusual.

I was very fortunate to be brought up in a supportive, outdoorsy environment where my sisters and I were encouraged to go outside just as much as our brother was. I am eternally grateful that my parents didn't restrict my participation in mountain-biking, or tree-climbing, or whatever else I got up to, and have struggled to understand why some people still see the outdoors as a male domain.

It's only relatively recently that I've realised just how few female role models I had, which is probably why I have a very clear memory from my first Alpine climb. I was in my late teens and had just summited a high glacial peak with a friend. When we got back to our accommodation, we read the guide to the climb we'd just completed. Guide books on Alpine mountains give detailed descriptions of a route, telling you where to expect difficulties and how hard and exposed it is.

What caught my attention was that the first descent of this mountain's north face − a 300-metre sheer cliff − had been achieved by a woman. According to the book, while on the summit she had dropped her purse into the valley below and had climbed down with her guide to retrieve it! It's hard enough climbing up that face let alone down it, but the really remarkable thing was that she did it in a skirt! She was probably wearing a corset too (which would have restricted her breathing) and would have drilled nails into the soles of her boots to gain enough purchase on the ice. The image of her in her finery holding a long Alpenstock ice axe was beautiful and inspiring. Since then I have been fascinated by old mountaineering photos: it turns out that many a woman balanced on a ladder spanning a crevasse or walked across an expansive glacier.

If you go looking for them, you'll find plenty of daredevil

women in climbing and travelling histories, but they're not as well-known as their male counterparts, which is a shame: they were remarkable women who did remarkable things. In the 1760s Jeanne Baret became the first woman to circumnavigate the globe and did so disguised as a man on a ship in the French Navy. Lady Hester Stanhope was a pioneering archaeologist who, in the early 1800s, explored the Middle East carrying a sword while riding a huge stallion; and in 1871 Lucy Wallace became the first woman to climb the Matterhorn, apparently living on a diet of sponge cake and champagne (I totally need to rethink my nutrition plan). The frustrations I sometimes encounter due to my sex aren't because of any outright bullying: they're more to do with the perception other people have about women in my profession because the stories of women like Jeanne, Hester and Lucy are so rarely told.

My sister Pippa recently reminded me that when I'd first started working for the bushcraft company in the Lake District, I'd told her I had to work twice as hard to be noticed in the same way as my male colleagues, or for some people to take me as seriously. Although it was irritating when a client instinctively asked a male instructor a question rather than me, I never let it put me off. Instead I took it as a challenge to show them I had just as much right to be there as anyone else. I wasn't the only one who didn't have female role models: they didn't either. If someone has only ever seen images of a man as a leader, that's what they think a leader looks like, but it doesn't mean they can't be educated by exposure to women in that role. I wonder if I found this prejudice easier than some to overcome because I never doubted or questioned my right to be there.

My sex has never defined me, and I don't know if being a woman is the reason why I have a different approach and leadership style from my male colleagues. I'm pretty flexible when I'm at work – I can adapt my style to suit the client or the type of expedition – but I'm not sure if that's to do with my sex or my personality. However, I am aware that there are times when clients respond differently to me because I'm female. People tend to open up to me far more than to some of my male colleagues. They seem to feel comfortable telling me about anything from swollen, infected mosquito bites on scrotums to domestic abuse. This gives me an advantage: if someone is hiding illness or masking fear, it can potentially put the rest of the team in danger. And now, because I've had so many such conversations, I'm really good at reading what people *aren't* telling me, which helps me address their needs and keep everyone safe.

I guess the fundamental reason why I don't see gender as particularly interesting is because the wilderness doesn't discriminate: it will kill a man as quickly as it will a woman, if you make the wrong decision. I know how important role models are, though, and feel proud and humbled (slightly embarrassed, too) now to be considered one. I occasionally get letters from fathers thanking me for being a great role model for their daughters, which is lovely: I remember feeling that I didn't fit the mould and feared being pushed down a path that wasn't for me. It's probably one reason why I was such a wilful teen, who skipped lessons and gave my parents a lot of grief. Perhaps if there had been someone like me in the public eye when I was growing up I'd have thought, Ah, it's OK, I can be like her. Looking back to when I started mountain-biking, I can't remember seeing another female riding, but now when I visit trail centres, there are often groups of women or mixed-sex groups. So much has changed for the better in just twenty years.

Although I love supporting and helping women gain confidence and find their place in the outdoors, I am just as intent on supporting men. I want to help as many people as possible, from every walk of life, to experience the wilderness. I feel so lucky to do such a wide range of work that allows me to share my passion for the wild. I never know what I'll be doing next. The next time my phone rings it could be a producer needing me to scout locations in the desert, or a director wanting me to set up abseiling stunts in the jungle. Or it might be a client asking me to plan an expedition that takes them deep into the bush or to the summit of Aconcagua. Putting together an expedition from scratch is like completing a complex puzzle: if you miss out one piece it could all fall apart: it's a challenge I really enjoy.

I lead corporate expeditions, too, taking co-workers on team-building adventures that test and challenge them. I work with young people, guiding school groups into extraordinary environments or showing groups of young entrepreneurs different ways to build their resilience and coping strategies.

No expedition is the same as the last and the skills I use can vary enormously. If I'm conducting survival training in a remote jungle, the soft skills of liaising with native peoples might be just as valuable as my knowledge of field medicine, and sometimes my ability to listen to a client going through a crisis will be the thing that keeps an expedition on track. I might be away for a week or for several months.

Whatever I do, whoever I work with, one aspect of my role is always the same: to encourage people to truly experience the wilderness, to find out what they're capable of, and to do it all as safely as possible. I'm so lucky to do something I love. I get to see amazing places, work with amazing people, and every day is different: I couldn't have planned it better if I'd tried.

2

The Modern Mind

In evolutionary terms, the time that's elapsed since our Stone Age ancestors were hunting with spears and living in caves is just a blip. In the past 10,000 years, human culture has evolved as we've acquired knowledge and skills, but our bodies have not. And because we're wandering round our urban, tech-filled planet with primal, animalistic brains, we sometimes respond unpredictably to modern life.

The threats we face today are not as obvious as the ones our ancestors dealt with, such as predators, starvation or dying from a flesh wound. Very often the biggest threats we face are to our mental health rather than our physical well-being as we wrestle with worries about job security, debt or finding somewhere safe to live. Despite this, we still produce a profound, evolutionary response to the sensory overload of our urban lives: stress.

When people get out into the wild – I see this particularly on bushcraft courses where there's more time for reflection, but also on mountaineering and climbing expeditions – something amazing happens: people suddenly feel able to talk about their emotions, perhaps especially when they're sitting around a camp fire. There's something about the flames dancing, the soft light flickering and chasing shadows that warms our souls as well as our bodies. Humans have been making fire for thousands of years, and as a consequence we have a deep, primal connection to it. We call it 'Bushman TV' because you can't help but stare at it. The modern mind, it turns out, isn't that modern after all.

The wilderness nurtures us, and soothes our stress, in ways that modern life often fails to do. It's not unheard of now for GPs to suggest exercise as a way of combating mild depression. Walking is beneficial because it releases endorphins, which make us feel better, and you also get a dose of vitamin D from sunlight, which lifts your mood. Going for a walk somewhere without a phone signal has another advantage: you get a break from the constant assault of social-media alerts and emails. The pressure of being 'always on' means spending time in nature has never been more therapeutic, which explains why more and more people are being drawn to experience what is, in an evolutionary sense, our natural habitat.

I often think about the stresses our ancestors must have

lived with. If they ran out of food, firewood or water, their lives were in danger. I try to imagine the anxiety they must have felt when eating foraged foods, unsure if they would be poisonous, or how they felt when they heard the roar of a predator. Stress, clearly, isn't a modern affliction, which is why we have such powerful physical reactions to it.

Picture a Stone Age woman coming face to face with a predator. Her stress hormones, mainly cortisol and adrenaline, would have been released, the cortisol to help her stay focused and motivated, the adrenaline increasing her heart rate, elevating her blood pressure and boosting her energy. Blood would have been diverted from her organs to her muscles so she could run or fight. Stress is actually a survival mechanism designed to kick-start our bodies in an emergency.

The problem is, we haven't yet evolved to deal with the constant stressors of modern life. Our primitive stress reaction isn't now triggered by short-term physical threats, like a predator, but by lingering pressures, such as work deadlines, relationship and family issues, even social-media posts. Every time we have a thought that threatens our well-being, the evolutionary stress response is activated because our bodies can't differentiate between real and perceived threats.

This puts a massive strain on our immune systems. Stressed people are more likely to have stomach problems, brain fog, depression and anxiety. Extended activation of the stress response (and the resultant exhaustion of the immune system) can lead to weight gain, autoimmune disease, ME, chronic fatigue and many other illnesses.

The real problem is that we no longer see stress as a wake-up call that something needs to change because it has become such a normal part of everyday life. If we were more in tune with ourselves we might recognise that a particular co-worker makes us feel uncomfortable, or that we always feel drained after checking Facebook, and we'd start to avoid them. If we were more in tune with our bodies we might realise we often feel bloated after eating a certain food, or depressed after drinking alcohol. But there isn't enough time in modern life to recognise the causes of our distress, and too many of us have become so accepting of how things are that we forget there may be an alternative.

Smartphones and social media have brought new anxieties into our lives – especially for young people – and that stress is almost constant. When I was at school you could get away from the bullies and the peer pressure when you got home, but children now live with them after school, at weekends and even during the holidays. They carry constant feelings of inadequacy because they're not only comparing themselves to their friends, but also to celebrities whose posts are carefully chosen (in some cases, Photoshopped) to make us jealous. Logically, we know it's daft to have the same reaction to a Facebook post as we do to nearly getting hit by a car, but our bodies produce the same 'fight or flight' response, no matter the source of the stress.

Of course, those pressures don't go away in adulthood. Too many of us experience debilitating emotions from trying either to excel or to fit in while also coping with genuine hardships, like family breakdowns, money worries or illness. And because there's no let-up, we're not reacting to stress in the way we used to. Our stress responses should be quick hits that help us identify threats and problems – our subconscious giving us a prod to make us take notice of something so we can either run from it or fight. But now that stress is so pervasive we no longer pick up on the signals, so we don't do anything to deal with its underlying causes. Meanwhile, the stress hormones are affecting our health.

There are other issues that make childhood today a very different experience from my own in the late eighties and early nineties. School playing fields have been sold off; children no longer walk or cycle to school, and they're not allowed to play out of sight of adults. Even their games have changed: I remember getting whacked on the hand by conkers (I confess to roasting mine to make them slightly harder), but some schools have banned them because they're worried about being sued if a child is injured.

I work a lot with youth groups and have noticed how many children are losing coordination and fine motor skills. Too many of the current generation are spending their lives indoors, playing on consoles and being burdened by homework. I also see plenty of young people who are being treated for depression, and many more who haven't been diagnosed, and I wonder if that has something to do with them being inside so much, constantly exposed to images of other people's 'perfect' lives.

When I was young, I was outdoors all the time. You ran,

you fell over, and you picked yourself up. You climbed trees, you dropped out of them, and you learnt how to move in the environment, but many of the children I work with don't have that. Sadly, I don't think those motor skills are something you can acquire later in life: there are some types of affinities and instincts that we best develop at a young age. Now that adult life is increasingly sedentary, some people never have the chance to find out what their bodies are capable of.

Other skills are being lost too. In the age of satnav, people are losing their sense of direction, of gauging how far along a route they are, or how to read a landscape. Perhaps most significant, in terms of how modern life shapes our thinking, is our expectation that if things go wrong someone will rescue us. We're so used to the idea that we can call the emergency services – or someone close to us – who will come and sort out our problems that some people who come on my expeditions can't comprehend that when things go wrong in the wild we really are forty-eight hours from help. They take unnecessary risks because they don't understand how serious the consequences can be. I often witness a general disconnection from the natural world, and a shocking lack of common sense. I've lost count of the number of times on expeditions in forests when I ask people to gather fire-wood . . . and they ask me where from!

It's no surprise to me that when people get out into the wild they feel better. It's not just that they're away from work, or out of phone range, they are reconnecting with something they sense is missing from their lives. It might not always happen instantly, but whether it takes a few hours or a few days, spending time in the wild changes people. Well, most people.

I always try to encourage my clients to fully experience the wilderness, but occasionally I come across someone who sees their adventure as something to Instagram or blog about. That saddens me because they're not fully experiencing the present moment. You can't properly take in the world's most amazing landscapes through a lens: you have to breathe them in, embrace them, and let yourself be taken over by them. I always point out things I find interesting in the hope of engaging others' imagination. Sometimes I'll even hire a local tribesperson to show us animals and plants that I wouldn't be able to spot. Every now and then, someone on an expedition is so focused on one particular goal, like reaching a summit or getting a shot of a golden eagle, that I have to push hard to make sure they notice anything else.

I love it when my clients have a goal – sometimes they give expeditions real focus and offer me a fresh perspective – but it's also important to me that they fully experience the amazing places I take them to: it's when you engage properly with the wilderness that you get the most from it. Time and again I see people transformed by their adventures, even if it sometimes takes things getting really tough to push them to find out who they are and what they're capable of.

I often get emails from clients months, or even years, after their expedition, telling me how their experience has empowered them to make changes in their life. What they learn in the wild they use at home and at work. You have no choice but to overcome challenges in the wild – you'll die if you don't – while in modern society it's sometimes possible to avoid confronting life's challenges, or wait for someone else to make the changes you want to see. In the wild, it all comes down to you. That's such a valuable lesson to learn because that's how you get the most out of life.

It's not just the modern mind that's becoming unsuited to the wilderness: our bodies are too. Many people now have jobs where they sit for most of the day; if they don't counteract this with exercise, it can cause problems like shortened hamstrings, stiff hips and a bad back. We're in danger of an entire generation losing the ability to move properly. It's always really obvious when I get clients who have been or are involved with martial arts, rock-climbing or dance. Even if they haven't done it for years, they move better than those who have never participated in sport.

People don't just return home fitter after an expedition: they go back to their jobs more alert and more responsive. Testing yourself in the wilderness exercises your brain as well as your body. The more you can stretch yourself, the more you use those mental and physical reflexes, the more likely you are to develop the mind of a survivor, whether that's at work, at home, or when it really counts in the wild.

3

Intuition

I have a friend who grew up around motorbikes and used to race speedway. He told me a story recently about watching a race while standing right next to the barrier. He was waiting for the bikes to come round the bend when something told him to move away. No more than a second later, a motorbike without a rider came hurtling round the bend, crashed through the barrier and landed where he'd been standing. If he hadn't moved, it would almost certainly have killed him.

We talked about what had made him move. He suggested there must have been something in the tone of the engine that told his subconscious something wasn't right. His brain was a depository of previous experiences around bikes and he knew the sound they should make if they came cleanly and safely round a corner. It must have been slightly different, which was enough for his subconscious to prompt him to move.

A few years ago, I experienced something similar. I'd been running a survival-instructor training course in Switzerland with my partner Stani and we were driving back to Chamonix where we lived. It was late, around 11 p.m., so we pulled over into a car park off a quiet road to cook some food. We got out our stove, heated a stew we'd made earlier in the day and sat down to eat it.

Stani was at one end of the bench while I was on the arm with my feet on the seat, facing him. As we were eating, a car pulled up behind me and parked at the other end of the car park, about forty metres away. A few minutes later I heard footsteps coming towards us and what happened next was bizarre.

The footsteps kept coming and, without a conscious thought, I leapt off the bench just as this guy reached for me with both hands. Stani instantly stepped in front of me and we both stood there, looking at this guy, who had bent down and was sniffing the spot where I had been sitting. When he looked up at us, his wild eyes were devoid of human emotion. I really felt as though I was staring into the eyes of a predator.

The tension was pierced a moment later by a shout from the other end of the car park: a second guy was calling to the first as if he was a dog. He took a final sniff before walking back to the car. I don't know what was wrong with him, whether he was on drugs or had mental-health problems, but it wasn't the kind of incident you forget.

Why had my intuition told me to move when I did? I've analysed it at length since, and I think the initial footsteps didn't trigger a response because they weren't hurried or unusual, just confident. But in a normal situation, if the person approaching was going to ask for directions, he would have paused or changed pace when he was near enough to introduce himself. When his footsteps didn't alter, it triggered my brain to realise something was wrong, prompting me to move at just the right moment to stop him getting hold of me.

Intuition is often described as a 'gut feeling' or a 'sixth sense', but it has a scientific root: it's your subconscious protecting you by using information you've stored from previous experiences, then sending a flare to your conscious brain. Neuroscientist Michael Gazzaniga estimates 98 per cent or more of all brain activity is completely unconscious. This includes controlling the functions that keep your body alive, like digesting food, keeping your heart beating and moving your muscles, but it also includes processing sensory input: the brain takes information from the world around us and makes it useful. We are bombarded by information from our environment, which, without filters, would overwhelm us, so we have evolved systems to protect us from the onslaught. One of those systems is our subconscious: it filters everything and only passes on crucial information to our conscious mind.

This is where intuition comes in. Your brain remembers the pain you experienced the last time you hit your thumb with a hammer, so it makes you pull your hand away to protect you from doing it again. Or it knows what a bike engine sounds like when it's out of control and makes you step away. These responses would have been useful to our caveman ancestors, alerting their conscious senses to movement in the bushes that let them know a predator or rival tribe was lying in wait.

This is why I always tell people in the wilderness that if something in their head tells them to stop, then stop! There's a reason your subconscious is sending you those signals. The more we tap into our intuition, the more we learn to trust it, and the more we make use of an extra resource that will keep us safe.

Because your subconscious is filtering so much information all the time, you may find your intuition works better when you're in a familiar environment. Imagine this scenario: you arrive home, open your front door and walk into your living room. You probably know if anyone in your household is at home without having to shout out. If you analyse why you know this, you might notice that something is out of place, or the heating is on, or you may just sense that you're not on your own. When you leave your front door in the morning, there will be days when you turn back to get an umbrella or a waterproof because you have a hunch it's going to rain. That's your survivor brain at work.

In an unfamiliar environment – like a survival situation

– we're processing so much information it may make us feel panicked so it is harder to tune into the signals our subconscious is sending. The way to combat this is by constantly testing the link between your subconscious and conscious brain so that you learn to trust your intuition.

The next time you go for a walk, whether it's in a city or through countryside, sit down for ten minutes and really pay attention to your surroundings. If you listen intently and observe carefully, you'll start to notice little things you normally walk straight past. I find what works for me is to take some deep breaths and exhale the thoughts that are taking precedence in my mind. I tune in to the environment around me and inhale the sounds, the smells, the wind direction and so on, one breath at a time.

In the wild, it might be something tiny that saves your life. Perhaps the way leaves rustle in a wind that can tell you a storm is coming or animal behaviour that shows a predator is near, but you don't have to be in a jungle to practise this: in your back garden there will be indications that something is about to change. Blackbirds, for instance, are very vocal and use a range of alarm calls depending on the threat, such as whether a predator is on the ground or in the sky. Squirrels also have a complex series of alarm calls that can sound either intense or anxious if you're able to tune in to them.

The more you observe, the more you'll learn. If you notice several animal tracks converging, your intuition will tell you that you're probably close to water. And if you really pay attention, you might even notice certain animals do certain things at certain times of the day. Pigeons, for instance, tend to drink in the evening: if you follow their lead at the right time of day, they'll be more likely to take you to water. This is the sort of 'intuition' tribal communities make such good use of because they have such a close relationship with their environment. If you were to spend as much time in their environment as you do at home, you would start to experience the same intuitive responses. The more you listen and observe, the more information you store for later use.

When I have time off, I'm always drawn to the mountains. I've been climbing since I was a child – I first walked up Snowdon when I was two, and when I was even younger I was carried on my dad's back – and in my twenties I lived for nine years near Chamonix in the Alps. It's the environment I'm most at home in so it's where my intuition is most effective. Over the years, I have acquired instincts about how the weather will change, or the angle of the terrain, or that a *whoomf* sound from the snow beneath my feet indicates an avalanche is more likely. But even my instincts, although pretty reliable, don't compare to those of indigenous mountain peoples, who have generations of wisdom and years of experience to enhance their intuition.

Exposure to a particular environment can help us hone our instincts, but with practice the instincts we acquire in one environment help us react in another. The more you pay attention to your intuition – in whatever environment – the more you'll trust it when it really matters.

We've all met people we just get a bad feeling about

when we're introduced to them for the first time. Often we don't know why we take against them, but we'll subsequently find out something about them that explains our initial reticence. There's a really good reason why we set such store on first impressions: it's because the greatest threat to us in the wild isn't the weather, or a mosquito, or a sheer cliff face – it's another human being. I'm currently planning a solo trip to Alaska and I'm much more concerned about coming across an isolated ranch, with a lonely rancher, than I am about encountering a bear. Sizing people up is part of our survival toolkit.

I get plenty of opportunities to test my intuition about people. Whenever I meet a new group of clients at the airport I can usually predict – from what they're wearing or how they're moving – what they'll be like on the expedition. The classic signs of someone who will struggle are that they're wearing brand new kit or not moving well. If they're a bit stiff, I know they'll find some of the terrain difficult, and when people find things hard and fall behind they can become moody or lash out. Noticing this early helps me guide them better and keeps the group together. In contrast, a really good sign is someone asking me how I am. It tells me they understand that, even though I'm there to do a job, and even though I'll always maintain a professional and positive exterior, I'm facing up to the same demons inside as everyone else. I don't consciously go around analysing people, but I suppose my subconscious is working out whom I can trust and whom I can rely on in a crisis, and that's just a normal intuition we all have.

So many of us are trying so hard to please, or to fit in, that we fail to recognise some pretty obvious warning signs about other people's character or behaviour. It can sometimes be hard to do in the moment, but on the train home or at the end of the day, you can hone your intuition by consciously making an inventory of whom you've met and if they displayed tell-tale signs you could have picked up on. If you don't trust someone, try to work out why. If you feel uncomfortable in a particular place, take a moment to figure out what's making you feel that way. The more you use your intuition, the more you'll trust it. And one day it might save your life.

It's not just the people you're with and your surroundings that send you subtle messages: your body does too. Take fear. It's often seen as a paralysing emotion, but it also serves an evolutionary purpose. Fear is a signal that something has changed. In the wild that may mean a predator, a storm coming or that the ground beneath your feet is about to give way. The more you recognise the messages your body is sending your brain – whether it's fear, cold, hunger or fatigue – the more insights you'll have to help you survive.

A few years ago, my intuition probably saved lives on an expedition I was co-leading in the jungle in Brunei. The other leader was ex-jungle warfare instructor and knew the area well because that was where they did their jungle training. It's harsh terrain, which was perfect for this expedition: our clients had signed up to be taught survival skills.

Whenever I set up camp in a jungle for myself or with

clients, I always go through the little mantra of 'look down, look up'. When I'm looking down, I'm searching for insects, water channels, any indicators that it might be dangerous to camp there. I look up because sometimes in jungles the trees are a hundred metres tall: if a branch has died up there but is being held in place by a vine, it could come loose in a gust of wind. Falling from that kind of height, it wouldn't have to be very big to do a lot of damage.

A few days into that trip, we were setting up camp for the night, and for some reason, I was much more meticulous about 'look down, look up' than normal. I didn't know why, but I was double-checking there were no dead trees anywhere near the camp, and when I was helping my clients get ready for the night, I was making sure all the knots were super-tight on their hammocks so that if the trees moved about in the wind there was no way they could work themselves undone. If the bashers – the tarpaulins that go over the hammocks – are even slightly loose, when the rain comes down (and in the jungle when it rains, it's like someone emptying a bucket over your head) it can end up channelling straight into your hammock and drenching your sleeping-bag. That night I didn't get into my own hammock until I was absolutely sure everyone's bashes were completely taut, checking even more thoroughly than I normally would.

Eventually I got into my hammock and went through the routine of 'powdering up'. In the jungle you are perpetually wet, either from humidity, sweat, wading through water or rainfall, and if you don't look after yourself your feet will start rotting within a matter of days . . . quickly followed by yeast growth in other nooks and crannies where you really don't want it.

I remember lying in my hammock, looking out at the night, listening to the cicadas and thinking how beautiful it was. I must have been asleep for a couple of hours when I woke up suddenly. It took me a moment to work out what had spooked me, and then I realised: the jungle had gone completely silent. The cicadas had stopped. That's when you know a storm is coming.

Insects are often your first clue that the weather is going to change, especially in a jungle where their background noise is so constant you only notice it when it stops. Insects are far more sensitive to change in atmospheric pressure that happens when cold and warm air mix, and it often silences them. It's so eerie it makes the hairs on the back of my neck stand up.

Just a few seconds after the cicadas had stopped, an icy blast of wind blew through our camp, followed by absolutely nothing. In another couple of seconds, the jungle went nuts. I've never seen trees bend so far, and all around us I could hear them falling over, crashing to the ground.

I'd been in quite a few jungle storms before, but nothing like that night's. When we got up in the morning the destruction made the place unrecognisable. There were fallen branches everywhere and I was glad I'd made sure that everything was tied down. I think we might have lost people if I hadn't.

I wouldn't be surprised if others in the group had also sensed that something was wrong because humans can detect changes in air pressure, if they pay enough attention. When people talk about 'the calm before the storm' they're actually sensing warm air being sucked down. Not only, on this occasion, did my subconscious pick up on that change, but I also had enough confidence in that environment to act on it. If other people had the instinct a storm was coming, perhaps they didn't feel it was their place to say anything. I'm willing to bet a similar dynamic happens in all kinds of workplaces when people have hunches that their company is making a bad move but wait for someone in authority, or with more experience, to raise the subject. I wonder how often people 'don't want to make a fuss' when they really should.

When we got back to our hotel at the end of the trip we heard that three guys on a jungle-warfare training course had died in the jungle that night. Experiences like that have taught me to listen to my intuition and, more importantly, to trust it. Over the years I've learnt just how powerful my subconscious is, and whenever I find myself instinctively doing something I can't quite explain, I don't have to wait many minutes before my conscious brain catches up with the threat.

4

Acceptance

In a real survival situation, panic can be your worst enemy. It is a normal response to finding yourself lost, or stranded, or injured, but if there's no one to help, you need to find a way to suppress it. If you can't control your emotions you won't be able to use your greatest asset – your mind – to its fullest capabilities.

It's pretty common when something goes wrong to want to blame someone for your predicament. 'If only we hadn't taken this path' or 'You should have packed that' or 'I should never have listened to so-and-so'. I hear this sort of thing all the time when expeditions don't go to plan. I call it 'going into victim mode', and if there's a time when you don't want to behave like a victim, it's when your life is on the line.

The best way I know of making sure you don't adopt this mindset is by accepting that bad things have happened to you: accepting your situation is the first step in dealing with it. You took a wrong turn. You didn't fill up your water bottle when you had the chance. You forgot to pack a penknife. Blaming yourself – or anyone else – won't help you. So, you took a wrong turn. Now what? So, your water bottle is empty. Where are you going to fill it? You don't have a penknife. What can you use instead?

Just as in everyday life, expeditions will throw curve balls at you: the weather may be too bad to go for the summit, or there's a political uprising, or maybe it's something as simple as someone becoming unwell, all of which are beyond the leader's ability to control. When expeditions don't go to plan, people may find that their trip of a lifetime has become one of the most stressful experiences of their life, which manifests as disappointment, anger and sometimes fear. Occasionally I'll have someone in my group who is so fixed on achieving their expedition goal – because it's their life's ambition – that they rail against the situation to the extent that they lose touch with reality.

You see it in everyday life too, whether it's the guy on the train fuming into his phone because there's a delay, or someone complaining in a restaurant because the kitchen got their order wrong. If they could keep a clear head, they'd be much more likely to resolve their problem quickly.

In the wilderness, irrational thinking impacts on your

survival chances because it stops you accepting your situation, which delays the point at which you can take back control. Of course, the same is true whether you're in the jungle, the mountains, or at work: raging against injustice only clouds your thinking.

I've noticed that those who reach acceptance first tend to be people who have been tested in other areas of their life. By the end of the expedition, I'll have learnt a lot about those I'm travelling with, and it's not a coincidence that the ones who have been through major life events, such as bereavement or illness, are often the ones who more easily accept that the expedition hasn't gone to plan. It seems their traumatic life experiences have made them more adaptable to, and more accepting of, change.

In order to survive we need to bring everything we have to the wilderness, and that includes our life experiences. Resilience is transferable: whatever happens to us, in whatever walk of life, can be useful preparation for a survival situation.

When someone really can't shake their victim mindset, one of the things I say to them, which sometimes helps, is that the wilderness is neutral. It doesn't have a personal vendetta against you. It doesn't care if you live or die. It's not your enemy or your friend. Once they realise the wilderness is not out to get them, and that the victimisation they're feeling stems from something internal, it helps them to accept that we are where we are. Instead of fighting something that we have no power to change at that particular moment, acceptance unsticks their thinking so we can move on.

As long as you feel sorry for yourself, or see yourself as a victim of circumstance, you won't be in a position to solve your problems. This is true in all kinds of other areas: how often have you felt that 'the establishment' doesn't care? Corporations, bureaucracies or computer glitches make life difficult for all of us from time to time, and although it might *feel* like they're waging a vendetta against us, our reaction says much more about our own stress and anxiety – how we feel about ourselves – than about how we're viewed by those entities.

I've noticed that younger people tend to respond more quickly to survival events, and I wonder if this is because they don't have such fixed ideas about how things are meant to be. One of the most famous survival stories concerns seventeen-year-old Juliane Koepcke, the sole survivor of a plane crash in the Peruvian jungle in 1971. She was travelling with her mother on a commercial flight that was struck by lightning and broke up in mid-air. Although a few other people, including her mother, had survived the impact, the debris was scattered over such a large area that Juliane was unable to locate them. After finding some sweets at the crash site – which would be her only food for the next nine days – she started following a stream in search of rescue. Juliane had spent some time in the jungle before the crash – her father worked as a researcher at a remote station – so she had a little knowledge, but that advantage was countered by the fact she had lost her glasses (she was very short-sighted), a shoe and was wearing only a flimsy cotton dress. She had also sustained several injuries in the crash.

It would be so easy in that situation to believe everything was hopeless, or to be so afraid, or so angry, that you'd see no point in even trying to get out. But Juliane took just a day to decide to leave the crash site and start walking. She accepted the enormity of what had happened to her extraordinarily quickly, which might have saved her life: without proper food, rest or clothing, the harsh environment and her injuries would have drained her resources quickly. It is even possible that if she'd waited another day, she wouldn't have had the cognitive function to make the huge decision to leave. Making it so quickly meant she retained enough physical strength to reach help in time.

Even when your life isn't on the line, acceptance and open-mindedness can help you get much more out of any situation. I shouldn't be surprised any more that clients sign up for group trips without realising that other people will be in the group. Some are so focused on having their own trip of a lifetime they don't understand that everyone is trying to do the same thing (or has a slightly different agenda). I can lead trips on which one person wants to hammer themselves and go as fast as possible, and someone else prefers to wander and take lots of photos. It can be a difficult situation to manage when you're leading a group solo, which is why I encourage people to accept that others may have different goals, different phobias, food intolerances, or whatever: when you're fighting each other, you can't truly experience the place you're in. The same applies when you're stuck working with people who have their own agenda. Unless you're going to work alone, or travel solo, you have to accept you're not going to get everything your own way. With the right attitude, however, you may discover that living within these boundaries leads to a different understanding of your environment, which can be surprisingly rewarding.

Acceptance enables you to ditch your emotional baggage and think more clearly because you're no longer sapping your energy fighting reality. It isn't about putting up with a terrible set of circumstances, sitting down and waiting to die: it's about not blaming anyone (including yourself) so you can start to think your way out of trouble. When you can't change the facts, your only option is to change your attitude.

Several years ago, on one of my first professional expeditions, I was spending time with the San Bushmen in Namibia. One morning I was packing away our tents in the back of the Land Rover and a scorpion dropped off the bottom of one onto my ankle. It stung me twice. Before it scurried off, I recognised it as the most poisonous scorpion in the country. I'd never seen anybody get stung by a scorpion before. I had no experience of it. All I knew was that it could be deadly. Initially it wasn't any worse than being stung by a bee, but it quickly became excruciating as the pain started to radiate away from the sting site.

My mind automatically told me, 'You can't panic because if you panic the blood's going to flow through your veins a lot quicker and then you've got less chance of survival.' When we feel anxious, our bodies release adrenaline, which makes our hearts pump faster to send blood to the areas we most need it. Our breathing gets faster so we can increase our supply of oxygen. This is great if you need to run for your life, but potentially fatal if you want to stop a deadly toxin reaching and damaging your organs.

Somehow, I was able to accept what had just happened, stay calm and find my boss. When I told him I'd been stung, he didn't believe me because I wasn't panicking. Thankfully, we had an expedition medic with a comprehensive medical pack, and he quickly hooked me up with intravenous anti-histamine, which saved me from a lot of pain and potential loss of consciousness, and might also have saved my life.

A similar thing happened last year. I was running the safety team for a corporate event in a remote corner of New Mexico. A car company was releasing a new 4x4 and they wanted to take a bunch of journalists and celebrities into extreme terrain to show off their new product. My job was to set up stunts and challenges for the celebrities while keeping everyone safe. We set up camp in a stunning location that also happened to be home to the extremely venomous coral snake. We were about a four-hour walk from our vehicles, then a three-hour drive to get medical assistance when I got bitten. It was almost as if it happened in slow-motion because I had enough time to watch the snake dislocate its jaw and I remember thinking, Oh, wow, that's really cool.

A fraction of a second later I realised it wasn't in any way cool: it was hanging onto my hand so tightly that I couldn't shake it off. I knew that if it was a coral snake I would die: medical help was impossible somewhere so remote. Unlike the scorpion in Namibia, though, I wasn't entirely sure what had bitten me – there's also a non-lethal mountain king cobra that looks exactly like the coral snake. Both have distinctive – and, frankly, sinister – black, red and white banding, and they're both quite small. There was just no way of knowing which had bitten me . . . unless and until I fell ill.

There is an anti-venom to treat every bite, but they are incredibly expensive, have a short shelf life and need to be kept refrigerated, so they're impractical to carry on expeditions. I knew the second I'd been bitten we wouldn't have any with us. And yet I still didn't panic, even though there was a 50 per cent chance I could be dead within a couple of hours. I also knew that, if it was a coral snake bite, I would have an incredibly painful death because their venom is neurotoxic, which means it affects the nervous system, inflicting paralysis and seizures. Other types of venom kill in different ways: myotoxic venom causes muscular necrosis (death of the muscle) and can also lead to kidney failure; haemotoxic venom destroys red blood cells and leads to organ failure; and cytotoxic venom affects cell tissues. If you're lucky, this will be restricted to the skin around the bite site.

We bound my hand, using a technique known as lymphatic wrapping, in which there is no tourniquet but restriction of lymphatic movement to try to keep the venom within the arm and away from the heart. Other than that, all I could do was wait.

My mind went to a really practical, logical place. I experienced clarity of thought and total acceptance of the situation. I'm not sure how or why I enter this state, but knowing how my mind reacts gives me an inner strength. I trust myself to control my emotions even if I cannot control the situation. Perhaps a part of me also knew panic wasn't an option because, if it had been a coral snake, there would be things I'd want to do, like passing messages to family and friends back home. I needed to be calm for that.

It was a half-hour wait: if I wasn't writhing in agony by then we could be sure it was a cobra bite. It was one of the few times in my career when there wasn't much I could do. After half an hour, I started to think I'd been lucky, and after an hour I knew I had.

I'm often asked what I feel after situations like that, when I've come close to dying, and the honest answer is not a lot. For starters, on an expedition there is always something else to focus on, so it's usually a question of 'So that happened. Now what do I have to do?' There just isn't the time to dwell on how close I came to death. But there's an underlying reason why my body and my mind recover quickly from near-death encounters: I accept that what I do is dangerous. I don't want to die, and I don't want to be severely injured, but I understand that what I do for a living comes with a lot of risk. I do everything I can to mitigate it, but there are some situations you can't do anything about.

Interestingly, I've noticed that, in the wild, people often find it easier to accept the things that are out of their control – like a boulder rolling down a hill towards their tent, or it being too wet to light a fire – than they do in their everyday lives. This is one of the greatest lessons the wilderness can teach us: bad stuff happens that isn't our fault. We look for reasons as to why we got ill, or why our boss is in a bad mood, and very often there just aren't any. And even if there is an explanation, there probably wasn't anything we could have done about it. Yet we spend so much energy beating ourselves up for not being where we want to be, or not living the life we hoped to live. The wild constantly reminds you that getting up in the morning is a risky business.

I suppose the crucial thing is – even if there was something you could have done differently – what really matters is how you get yourself out of the place you're in. Apportioning blame to a colleague who 'stole' your promotion or berating yourself for choosing the 'wrong' degree doesn't help you, any more than arguing about who couldn't read the compass properly stops you being lost!

Acceptance can help you move on emotionally too. When a relationship has run into difficulties, too often couples will look to blame each other for what's gone wrong, or cling too tightly to memories of how things used to be, which prevents them acknowledging that – for whatever reason – it's probably time for them to move on from each other. Such acceptance will come with a lot of heartache, but the pain is accompanied by immense relief and is, hopefully, followed by excitement as new possibilities emerge. In the wild, acceptance can save your life. It may not have quite such dramatic benefits at home or at work, but it can still be the starting point for getting what you need or want out of life.

I learnt a really big lesson about just how valuable acceptance is from a colleague of mine, Steven Ballantyne. He was working in Papua New Guinea about thirty years ago when he was in his twenties. He knew that there were some tribal battles going on in the area where he was trekking, and one day some guys popped out of the bushes with AK-47s. He knew there was nothing he could do to save his life, apart from surrender, and instantly got down on his knees, raised his hands and lowered his head: a complete demonstration of submission. He didn't try to fight, or attempt to run, just handed himself over. He believes that that total acceptance of his situation saved his life. He knew the tribes in the area had very high moral standards and they wouldn't fight an unarmed person if you didn't give them a reason to do so. Steven was held hostage for ten days, eventually escaping with the help of two women from the tribe.

Acceptance is an important survival trait because it isn't just about getting yourself out of a life-threatening situation: it's about not getting into one in the first place. When you make camp for the night, you are usually exhausted, probably hungry and dehydrated, maybe a bit sore from blisters or pulled muscles, and either very cold or too hot. When you're that vulnerable, especially when it gets dark, you have to accept that there are certain things you can't do: whatever it is will be better tackled in the morning after some rest, and when it's light. I have a really strict rule on my trips that we don't use knives after dark. Sharp tools – knives, axes, machetes – are the workhorses of expedition life and are used for everything from cutting trails to splitting firewood to preparing food. Despite their usefulness, it's simply too dangerous to use them when it's dark. When everything's against you, why create more risk? Even if you're working by the fire, you can't always see because the flames flicker. It's not just that you risk injuring yourself, it's that if you do hurt yourself you're so far from help that it won't arrive in time. In some of the terrain I work in, I may be just a few miles from a medic as the crow flies, but the ground is so steep, so wet or so completely covered with undergrowth that it would take a day or two to reach help. That kind of terrain also makes it impossible for a helicopter to land. It's simple: no cutting after dark. It's just one of the things you have to accept.

A few years ago, I was co-leading a group of twelve on an expedition in the Arctic. After we had made camp, one of the men in the group started chopping firewood with an axe. I didn't get a chance to stop him before he put the axe head through his boot. It had a thick rubber outer and a thermal felt liner and this had been enough – or so we thought – to stop the blade reaching his foot. In the dark it was hard to tell but as he wasn't in any pain it seemed he'd had a lucky escape. Our biggest concern was that snow would get inside the boot and cause frostbite. But about an hour later he said he was feeling tired and was going to his tent. He stood up and immediately passed out. It was only when we took his boot off that we found the axe had gone through his foot, which had been bleeding into his boot. It sounds mad that he didn't know he'd put an axe through his foot, but I've cut myself with a knife a few times and not realised it. When your brain is focusing on other things, as it often is in the wild, it doesn't always prioritise pain signals coming from your peripheral nervous system, signals that can also be slowed in extreme cold.

It took us five hours to get him medical help. Had we been anywhere more remote he would have died. If he'd cut an artery it probably wouldn't have mattered if we'd only been an hour from a hospital because he'd have bled to death in that time. When I'm teaching knife work, I get beginners to put their elbows on their knees when they're sitting down as that more or less stops the chance of your blade going into the femoral artery in your leg: if you put your blade through that, there's very little anyone can do. It's under the same sort of pressure as a fire extinguisher and you can bleed out very quickly. The only thing you can do is literally push your fingers into the wound and pinch the ends of the artery. But if the cut is near your groin, the end can retreat up into the torso: unless that happens in an operating theatre, there's not much hope. In a wilderness setting, there's no way you could save someone.

Which is why accepting what you can't do is as important as accepting what has happened. The next step is doing something about it.

5

Curiosity and Creativity

People are often surprised when I tell them these twin traits are two of the most important components of the survivor's mindset. I believe that if you can access and utilise both, you've got a very good chance of making it out alive: curiosity will help you explore your environment, and creativity will ensure you get what you need out of it.

There's a well-known mantra in survival circles: improvise, adapt and overcome. If you ever find yourself in a disastrous situation you can pretty much guarantee that you won't have your knife, your water bottle, your fire-starting kit or your book on edible wild plants with you. All you'll be likely to have are the clothes you're wearing and whatever is in your pockets or handbag. In that scenario, you'll need curiosity and creativity to improvise your way out of trouble.

Stani and I have just returned from a trip to the USA, and after we'd cleared the rigorous security screening we were sitting in the departure lounge. Anything most people would consider useful in a survival situation was in our checked-in bags and all we had with us was the normal hand luggage of the average traveller – phone, laptop, wallet, headphones, keys, book, notepad, pen, small tube of toothpaste and a toothbrush – yet we counted eleven ways to start a fire with what we had on us and what we could see around us. We could have taken the battery out of our phones, stripped the wire from our headphones and held the wire against the contact points on the battery. That would create a glowing ember we could use to ignite tinder we could make from shredding pages of the notepad. Or I could have taken the screen off my phone and used it as a lens. In other circumstances I could have broken the screen and used it as a blade, or stripped down my charging cables to make a small animal trap or a fishing line . . .

Real survival requires you to make use of everything you've got, and that means extending your curiosity to yourself. What inner resources can you exploit? Maybe you're a keen ornithologist and know about the behaviour of certain birds that could lead you to water. Or maybe in your GCSEs you learnt about the 'fire triangle', how a fire needs three things to burn: fuel, heat and oxygen. Even if you've never made a fire, these snippets of information are resources that, along with a bit of creativity, could get you out of a crisis. You'll be surprised by how much you have actually learnt over time.

The guy sitting next to you will have skills too. What has he got and how best can his talents be put to use? Maybe your greatest asset is your ability to talk to people and encourage them to come forward. The more you communicate, and the more curious you are, the more you'll discover interesting and useful things.

One of my roles on some film shoots is to come up with new – and totally wacky – ways to survive. Producers are always looking for original footage and stunts viewers have never seen before. People watching might laugh at some of the ideas, but everything I suggest is something I would genuinely do in a worst-case scenario. I remember on one episode of *Man vs Wild*, Bear gutted a seal so that he could wear the skin as a gilet. It sounds ridiculous, but this was in a remote part of Scotland and it meant he had all that blubber – which seals have evolved so they can spend long periods underwater – insulating him from hypothermia. Most people would walk straight past a seal carcass, but even the most unlikely objects can be life-preserving, if you think about them in the right way. (If you do come across a seal carcass, don't forget the gut can be used in place of a rope, you can smear the fat over your skin as sun cream, and with the right tools, the skin can be used to make clothing or even a canoe!) When I am in a survival scenario, as soon as it becomes safe to do so I take stock of everything I have on me, because even the most mundane objects might provide the key to my getting out.

When Stani and I are on long, boring road trips, we'll often amuse ourselves by saying, 'What have you got in your pockets right now you could use for survival?' It's really good fun, and it's a great game to play with children because they come up with crazy and innovative ideas adults wouldn't even consider. There are no wrong answers, and the great thing is that using your brain in this way keeps it flexible and alert.

Did you know, for example, you could use a lipstick to waterproof small items such as matches? Or you could use it to write a message? Or as a lubricant? If it's been made with petroleum jelly you could even use it as a fire starter. Awesome! Condoms have loads of potential not related to their intended purpose: you can carry water in them, use them to keep small items dry, as a rubber glove if you're dealing with blood or body fluids, as a tourniquet or a sling shot. They're also super-flammable and can be used to light a fire in the wet. When it comes to survival there are no rules: just because you know an object is intended for a specific purpose, it doesn't mean it can't be used for something else. You have to use whatever you've got, and that includes your imagination.

I have a twenty-month-old nephew, and it's been fascinating to watch him explore his world. He does it by tasting things and hitting things and opening things: his curiosity is helping him discover not just his world but what he's capable of.

And each time I see him he's capable of a little bit more.

I see it to some extent in my dog too. Tug is a two-year-old part-Siberian husky, with primal instincts to chase, hunt and run. She needs a lot of stimulation (which is why, although they're very loving dogs, it can be cruel to keep one if you can't give it the attention it needs). As a puppy Tug pushed hard and was a real challenge. I was keen for her to roam off the lead, but that meant she had to respect and trust me, and respond to my commands. Now she's growing older, she's still challenging me and my boundaries, and occasionally refuses to come when she's called. Sometimes she'll sit down and look at me as if she's giving me the furry middle finger: 'So, Human, what are you going to do about this?'

Curiosity seems to me to be an inbuilt evolutionary trait in all animals. One of the most remarkable things I ever experienced was nearly having a tortoise land on my head! It had been dropped by an eagle, which had learnt that the only way to break the shell was to let it go from a great height. Think of the curiosity and creativity it took to work that out, or how much experimentation it took for chimpanzees to discover they could use sticks to harvest ants from inside their nests. That tells me curiosity is evolutionary, which means it must serve a purpose in our survival.

There's a reason why toddlers need to empty the cereal box all over the floor: it's to see what happens and to gauge how their parents react. If we weren't curious about climbing stairs, we wouldn't figure out how to do it. However, if you fast-forward a few years, curiosity and ingenuity are all too often forgotten in children's development. When I was teaching outdoor education at the school in Switzerland, I worked with some of the most privileged children in the world – their parents were ambassadors, CEOs and royalty. By the age of nine or ten they were capable of holding very adult conversations about finance or literature, even the meaning of life, but they didn't really know how to play.

The school had an amazing outdoor programme that included taking children skiing, rock-climbing and mountaineering, and teaching them survival. I took a group of younger children camping and it struck me that they didn't know how to explore. It was almost as if they didn't know they *could* explore. When I was young, I was out building dens and going on arduous expeditions to the end of the garden with my brother and sisters. We'd be fighting crocodiles or crossing imaginary rivers, but with the pupils in Switzerland I had to structure their play, organising games of Capture the Flag or even something as basic as Hide and Seek.

Over the course of a term, I was able to take a step back and gradually their capacity to make up their own games blossomed. After a couple of years' working with them, all I had to do was establish the perimeter of where they could safely go, then let them run off to explore, sometimes for hours at a time. It was wonderful to see, but what was even more awesome was how they absorbed newcomers into the fold and showed them how to play too. Now that so much of school life is about adhering to a prescribed curriculum and passing exams, I worry that creativity is being shut down in a generation of children.

Increasingly, we live in a goal-oriented culture with expectations that we'll take a pre-determined route through life. That leaves too little room for self-discovery and creativity and closes our minds to other possibilities and opportunities. It's almost as if it creates a kind of tunnel vision about our lives that stops us developing other talents, instincts and ambitions.

At home, it can be so much easier to sit a child down with a PlayStation or Xbox than to encourage creative play – it takes time working parents don't have. That means children are spending time with someone else's imagination rather than developing their own. Curiosity is such a fragile trait: it needs to be supported and nurtured. When a child asks a question, the answer they're given can expand their world and move the boundaries of what they think is possible. When adults don't have the time to give adequate answers, they squash that child's enthusiasm for asking questions, which in turn stops them exploring their world.

I know a lot of parents and carers worry about taking children outdoors, and I'm often asked about ways to do it safely. The answer, more often than not, is to let the child lead. See what they're interested in, look where they're looking, then answer their questions. So long as you set safe parameters and use your common sense, don't worry too much if they fall over: finding out how much things hurt is a really good way of testing their boundaries. And if you don't know the answer, make up something magical and engage their imagination. You won't just be creating lifelong memories, you'll be shaping a more confident, creative person. I've never forgotten something brilliant my father told us when we were children. There is an old gas lamp that stands alone on the Malvern Hills. Apparently it inspired part of *The Lion, the Witch and the Wardrobe*, and Dad told us that when we touched it he couldn't see us! It was so simple, but it opened up a whole range of magical possibilities for us to enjoy.

As adults, we have so much to gain from going out into the wild with children because they help us see things we might have stopped looking at. Constantly asking yourself questions like 'Why does that grow there?' or 'Why have the birds stopped singing?' may one day provide answers that will save your life.

Quite early on in my TV career, I was asked to help out on the pilot of a TV show about the first seventy-two hours of survival. It's often said that if you can survive the first seventy-two hours after a disaster, you have a very good chance of making it home. This crucial period is when you put creativity into practice and escape, or you gather enough information about your new environment to survive there. The idea of the show was to put contestants into a plane-crash situation (so they'd have only the clothes they stood up in and a knife, if I remember correctly) to see if they could get to a designated extraction point within seventy-two hours.

The location – the Kruger National Park in South Africa – had already been chosen, so my job was to be the guinea pig and prove it was possible to survive in that environment. I wasn't being followed by a film crew, but I had a GPS tracker with me so I knew I was a red dot on a computer screen somewhere. The tracker had an emergency button, which, when pressed, would normally send a signal to the GEOS international emergency response centre with my GPS coordinates, but this one had been adapted to send a signal to the base camp a few miles away. Other than that, I was completely alone. All I had was a knife, a small medical pack and a litre and a half of water.

It was 38–39°C when I was dropped into the area by helicopter, so I knew my priority had to be finding water. However, I felt such a huge amount of pressure to prove I knew my stuff that I got off to a really bad start. I had sold myself as a survival expert and had an overwhelming feeling of 'I cannot fail at this. I just can't.' I was new to TV, and didn't want to let myself down, or show myself up, and that pressure – all of which I put on myself – created feelings of panic that manifested in tunnel vision. I was so focused on what was in front of me that my peripheral vision actually started to blur. It wasn't long before I was making quite bad decisions.

In the midday sun, with very little shade, I started crossing the stretch of scrubby desert. I'd been told there was water out there – I had to prove that it was possible to find water – and I guess I felt that, as a so-called expert, I should be able to locate it easily. But all I was doing in that heat was accelerating dehydration. A complete amateur.

I was putting so much pressure on myself that the tunnel vision got worse: I became so incapable of exploring the landscape, of asking the right questions about what was in front of me, that I was putting my life in danger. I eventually got to the point where I had to tell myself I was being ridiculous: I was more than capable of doing this – I had done so on numerous occasions before. I just needed to stop and assess the situation.

I found some shade under a bush, sat down, drank some water and gave myself a really tough talking-to. 'Right, Meg. This is all about tactics, and it's about utilising the environment the best you can. You know how to do this. Stop dicking around and start looking for clues.'

After that, my mind started slowly to open up and I began to explore the environment by looking, listening and thinking. I also remembered I needed to rest until the sun was lower in the sky to conserve my water. In the distance there was a small mountain range, and I decided that – when it got cooler – I would head towards it: a change in geology like that can indicate softer rock coming up against harder rock, which can force water to the surface.

After a couple of hours, I started walking and began to notice several animal tracks. I soon realised they were converging, so I asked myself why. The obvious answer was that the animals had found water, so I followed the tracks. Sometimes you'll find standing – or, if you're really lucky, running – water, but a dried puddle is more likely. You may think that means the water has run out, but if the puddle happens to be at the bend in the meander of a dry river bed, you may be in luck. When the water flows around a bend, most of the water gets channelled to the outside, which means this is the last part of the ground to dry out. Occasionally, creeks continue to flow underground, and if you dig down in those damp patches, you are rewarded with a trickle of running water.

More and more, my brain was making connections between the things I was seeing and the meaning behind them. At first I noticed lizards sunbathing on rocks, which told me there had to be insects in the area for them to eat, and then I stumbled across a bee, which was really encouraging. Bees are a good indication that water is nearby: they need water to control the humidity and temperature of their hive. As they rarely store it, it had to mean I wasn't too far from a supply.

So I followed the bee, but instead of it leading me to water I ended up beside a dead tree. It wasn't very big, probably about fifteen feet tall, and I could see the bees had made a nest in the top. That meant one thing: honey. I knew I wasn't allergic to bee stings, so I looked for wood I could use to make a hand drill.

By rubbing together two pieces of wood – one on the ground, and a stick whittled to a dull point that you rotate quickly between your palms – you can create enough friction in such arid conditions to generate an ember, which can ignite a bundle of dry grass. My plan was to smoke the bees out and make them sufficiently drowsy that I could stick my hand in and take the honey. Without protective clothing I still got stung, but not by nearly as many bees as I would have done without the smoke.

Not only did that honey give me energy, it also gave me confidence that I knew what I was doing and that I had what it took to survive. I loved that my curiosity had helped me find the honey, and that my creativity had allowed me to get hold of it. But honey wasn't going to keep me alive: I still needed water.

The first source I found on that trip was in the grooves of another tree. It was a way of collecting water I had first learnt from spending time with the San Bushmen. Rain and dew can collect in the grooves of bark at the Vs where branches form, and when I saw dark patches on tree trunks I knew they had to be holding some water. You can siphon it into a container or you can drink straight from the hollow if you can find a straw. I looked around for hollow grasses and reeds and was able to rehydrate a little.

The physical benefit of finding water was as important – in that particular situation – as the psychological. It's the most incredible feeling when you create a little success story in places like that, and I believe it's really important to celebrate those little victories. It may be a British trait to play everything down, but being able to congratulate yourself on finding what you need, knowing you've given yourself a few vital more hours of survival, boosts your confidence so that you keep seeking out other things that will lead you home. Don't see it as a tiny puddle: see it as the means to sustain your existence. Claim it. Celebrate it.

I always try to carry with me a pot: how else are you going to boil or carry water in the wild? Working with native tribes has shown me there are several ways. The Iban tribes in Borneo, for instance, were the first people I saw who used bamboo to carry water. Bamboo is segmented, and if you cut it in the right place and make holes to thread a cord through, you can make a kind of water shoulder-bag.

You can even boil and purify water in bamboo, if the wood is thick enough not to burn too quickly (and you have a way of holding it the right distance from the flames). I've seen the Iban and the Kelabit people steam rice and cook eggs – perfectly! – in bamboo segments. Once you know that, you start to look for other resources that have functions you don't immediately recognise.

But if you don't have a pot, and you're not in a place where bamboo grows (or you don't have a machete to cut it), what can you collect water in? How about an ostrich egg? It sounds implausible, but I've seen the San people make a little hole in the top, just big enough to get a straw in; they suck out the egg – a great source of protein – then use a funnel to pour in water, or hold it underwater. Ostrich eggs are pretty big, and fairly strong, and can carry several litres. Tribes like the San have given me so many lessons in creativity and ingenuity, which has shown me that – even if you can't see it at first – there will be something in your environment to help you.

I'm always on the look-out for rubbish because you'll usually find something useful. Old tyres or rubber shoe soles make great fire starters even in the wet (I always carry sections of old inner tubes when I'm working in damp conditions), and plastic bottles are great for carrying water. If you're lucky you'll find an empty metal tin, which is perfect for boiling water, but it might be that you have to improvise a way of carrying water. Can you strip bark off a tree and create a kind of basket? If you can do that, maybe you can line it with moss, seaweed or beeswax and make it as watertight as possible. Or can you soak your clothes with water, then wring them out into your mouth? If you really think about it, if you let loose your curiosity and your creativity, you'll come up with ideas that will sustain (and quite possibly entertain) you.

However, there are situations in which you should rein in your curiosity. In a survival situation, unless you have knowledge of a particular plant or animal species, you really shouldn't be eating it. You've got to hope that your immediate crisis is only going to last for a few days. As your body can go for around three weeks without food, you're actually putting yourself in more danger by eating something you're unsure of. If you make yourself sick, you'll lose a lot of energy very quickly, and if whatever you eat makes you vomit and gives you diarrhoea, you'll lose vital fluids. Even if the poison doesn't kill you, the dehydration it leaves in its wake might mean you don't survive long enough to get help.

There was a really great film a few years back called *Into the Wild*. It was based on the true story of Christopher McCandless, who left society behind and went walking all over the US. He ended up in Alaska when, according to his diaries, he decided to return to civilisation and started walking towards the nearest town, until his path was blocked by a river in spate. He was trapped. He took shelter in an abandoned bus and this was where, several months later, moose trappers found his body.

The journalist who wrote the book the film was based on speculated that McCandless had inadvertently poisoned himself by eating seeds from the wild potato plant. Although they don't always prove fatal, they would have weakened him to such an extent that he could no longer go out and forage. It is possible that curiosity had led him to eat the thing that caused his death.

In certain ancient cultures, like the Mayan and the Aztec, people who died in the search for plants with edible or medicinal properties were considered martyrs because they helped the tribe expand its knowledge. Trying new things might benefit society, but if it's just you the risks may be too great. You won't have a second chance if not and there isn't an emergency service in the wilderness to save your life.

You might – pretty sensibly – think that if you see Animal A eating Animal B then Animal B must be safe to eat. But in any given ecosystem, animals will have evolved together over hundreds of thousands of years: there are spiders that can digest some of the most poisonous frogs in the Amazon because they've adapted to process the toxins. You can't assume that because one animal eats another, or a berry or a fruit, that it's not poisonous.

If you've survived for a couple of weeks, then you will probably need to prioritise finding food. The safest things to go for are lizards, insects and fish. You won't like the taste of leeches, but they're unlikely to do you any harm if cooked (and once they're fried they're not too bad). As far as I know, there aren't any poisonous rodents, and all freshwater fish are safe to eat, so long as you remove the gut and cook them to kill parasites and bacteria. I'd stay clear of all berries and fungi, unless I was very sure of what I was looking at.

There are even times when having too much knowledge won't help you. If you look at some SAS survival manuals, you'll see all sorts of ingenious ways to find water, but the reality is you'll lose far more fluid through sweat by digging a well in the desert than you'll replace if you finally hit water. It can be true of food sources too: you could easily end up expending more energy finding and preparing some animals than you'd get back in calories. Survival is often about conserving energy so the smart thing is to find methods that do the work for you. Making hooks and fishing lines that you can put out in the water overnight, for instance, lets the river do the hard work while you rest (though I should point out that certain types of fishing, including setting night lines, are illegal in the UK, in part because they're so efficient).

This is why I say survival has more to do with brain than

brawn. I see the mind as a muscle, and to keep it working well it needs to be strong and flexible, which means you should start its new fitness regime right now. What's in your pockets? What's right in front of you? Now work out what you can do with those things. Then work out another use. And another. There are no wrong answers so have fun with it. Be outrageous. Be playful. Your first answer may not work, but it may lead you to a solution that does. And that may be the thing that saves your life.

6

The Active Mind

I said right at the beginning of this book that three seconds without thinking is enough to kill you. If you can find ways of keeping your brain active, of not switching off, it will have a bigger impact on your survival than if you've learnt how to make fire with a hand drill.

You might reasonably think that the best guide you could have on an expedition is someone who spends every day in their specialist environment. You'd probably feel even safer knowing nothing had ever gone wrong on a particular leader's expeditions. If you could, you'd probably choose a guide who takes clients up the same mountain day in, day out, especially if nothing bad had ever happened. If one day there's an avalanche and several of that guide's party are killed, you can almost predict what people are saying: 'He was such an experienced guide, it could have happened to anyone.' But, actually, there's a pretty good chance the guide had become complacent and fallen into what's known as a heuristic trap. He wasn't expecting change, so he'd stopped thinking about the environment around him, which meant he wasn't aware of anything changing. We're all vulnerable to thinking 'it's never happened before' so we don't even consider certain possibilities.

Heuristics are hard-wired mental shortcuts that everyone uses every day in routine decision-making and judgement. Familiarity breeds trust, and if something has worked before, we're more likely to do it again. This saves us time and frees our brain for other tasks. Heuristics are so powerful that advertisers and marketeers use them to make us buy their products. If you're in a supermarket, you'll see that cheaper brands are often designed to look like the premium ones – 'This is just like the brand you've been choosing all your life.' You can fall into a heuristic trap in any walk of life: think how often a fresh pair of eyes at work will spot something you may have overlooked because you've been dealing with it for so long. In the wilderness they can be really dangerous.

You are more likely to fall into a heuristic trap when you rely only on your previous experience of an environment to keep yourself out of trouble. In the wild, there are lots of variables. So much is out of your control that you must stay alert and keep your mind active so you'll spot the changes that are flagging up potential dangers.

Whether I'm on my own or with friends, whether I'm doing safety for a TV show or leading an expedition, I am constantly running scenarios in my head. What happens if one of my clients falls over on that loose shale? How would I get them out? What could I use as a splint? Or maybe I'll be thinking a little further ahead: what if the bridge over the river has been washed away? How will we cross? If we go upstream the river will be narrower, but if we go downstream we're more likely to find a boat. I'll be thinking about the weather, where we'll make camp, what we'll find to eat, or what happens if we hear gunfire. All the time. Constantly.

Sometimes my scenarios are totally crazy, like what would happen if a plane crashed in front of us (I once found myself mentally planning for an alien invasion – I put it down to the in-flight film), but it keeps my mind active and helps prepare me to deal with any eventuality. It also allows me to have a little fun: what if the zombies move quickly, like in *World War Z*, or slowly, like in *The Walking Dead*? How would that affect my tactics? After a month of leading an expedition you get tired, this sort of thinking combats exhaustion and fatigue. This kind of planning has another benefit: if you are constantly playing the role of problem-solver in your scenarios, it boosts your confidence and makes it even more likely you'll react positively when you need to.

My scenario planning is almost always of the worst-case kind, and if my clients knew about it they'd probably think I was being morbid. But it keeps my mind flexible, a vital attribute: when things go wrong on expeditions, they tend to go wrong in quite odd ways. The quicker you react, the less likely it is that the situation will escalate. The next setback is always going to be different from the last, and even if the same thing goes wrong, the solution is almost certainly going to be different: if your GPS unit fails, for example, you'll be able to navigate using the sun or the stars in some places, but if you're in the middle of dense jungle or thick fog, you'll need to rely on a compass or listen for aural clues, like the sound of water or nearby roads.

There's a saying in the adventure business: you don't plan for the 99 per cent of times that things go well, you plan for the 1 per cent when they don't. People need rescuing mostly because they didn't prepare for things to turn out any other way than perfectly. Thousands of people do the Tour du Mont Blanc – a hundred-mile trek through the Alps – every year, and when the weather's fine it's straightforward, even easy. All you have to do is follow the signposts (or the other people on the route). It's hard to go wrong, but if the weather turns bad, it's amazing how many people get lost because they can't see the path, let alone the signposts.

You may think you'd be able to tell if the weather was about to change, or that you'd get a warning to turn back, but sometimes the weather alters unbelievably quickly. If you don't have a plan about what to do when visibility is down to virtually zero, there's a chance you'll make a decision that could prove fatal. My scenario-planning means I'll have studied the map, memorised escape routes and worked out how I'll get my crew or clients down safely.

I enjoy coming up with scenarios. It can be quite exciting to wonder what I've got in my bag to use if somebody fell off the path right in front of me or to plan how I'd get down the cliff to them. How would I stabilise the situation? How would I call for help? How would I use things from the environment around me to improve matters? I pride myself on having the ability to deal with situations like that. Some of that confidence obviously comes from experience, but constantly running scenarios means I've always got a couple of courses of action to take the second something goes wrong.

One of the most famous survival stories of recent years was featured in the award-winning film *Touching the Void*. British mountaineers Joe Simpson and Simon Yates were descending from the summit of Siula Grande Mountain in Peru when Joe fell and broke his leg. Knowing rescue was all but impossible, the pair decided to lower Joe on a rope, but when – in the middle of a raging storm – he fell into a crevasse, Simon's only option was to cut the rope. If he hadn't, he'd have been pulled into the crevasse himself, or died waiting for rescue. It was a terrible decision to have to make but, having processed all the ways in which their desperate scenario would pan out, Simon did the only thing he could to save himself. Incredibly, Joe had survived the fall and, despite his injured leg, five days later he crawled into base camp, just hours before Simon would head back to civilisation.

Simon had a few minutes to make his decision, but often you have only seconds to come up with a plan. Sometimes even less. A while ago, I was rock-climbing with two friends in the Alps. We were roped together, with me in the middle, in a really rocky gully traversing a sheet of ice with a cliff below us that dropped hundreds of feet. Above us, a mountain guide was leading his party through a gully, dislodging stones that were raining down on us. We shouted up and told him he needed to move higher, but he didn't change his route. A few minutes later, a rock tumbled down and hit the friend in front of me, knocking him over and sending him spinning backwards down the cliff face.

There was probably five metres of rope between the two of us. I don't know what that corresponds to in time, but I must have had less than a second to react before all three of us would have wound up at the bottom of the cliff. As he had been moving in front of me, I'd seen him step over this small pinnacle of rock. Now I dropped to the ground and wrapped my arms round it. The friend behind was able to tie the rope to the rock and we pulled the other back up.

The point of these two stories is that it's one thing to have an active mind and to be constantly alert to danger and solutions, but you also need the instinct to react. Muscle memory plays an important part because sometimes your body will react before your brain has made a conscious decision. I know that when I'm short-roping (an Alpine technique that involves holding someone on a short rope to safeguard them) a nervous client or a camera operator who is focused on filming the action, my body reacts the instant they slip or stumble: not only do I hold them, but my body automatically puts itself in the strongest position to absorb their fall and either keep them on their feet or channel them to a safe landing. Those physical and mental reactions improve with experience, but as most people aren't constantly exposed to icy cliff faces, how do you test those instincts and your ability to take action? I honestly believe you can do it anywhere.

The next time you're driving, imagine what you'd do if that pedestrian stepped out, or the car behind overtook, or a motorcycle nipped up the inside. Or at work, what would happen if the woman at the next desk collapsed or you got stuck in the lift? The more you run scenarios in your head, the more you'll get a sense of what's likely to work and what's outlandish, but the very fact that you've been exercising your brain in that way makes it far more likely that you'll be one of the people to respond first. Athletes often talk about 'visualisation' where they envisage achieving a goal. This is usually very specific – jumping higher, throwing further – but your brain can play the same trick, making you believe that you are capable of achieving something you've never done before.

An active mind is particularly vital in my TV work. One week I'll be in a desert looking for water courses, the next in a jungle, wondering how we can get a shot of a presenter abseiling through a waterfall: I need to be able to adapt quickly, often while jet-lagged and enduring eighteen-hour days under pressure.

We work with the people in front of the camera and

behind it, helping the teams to set up their equipment and adapting it to the conditions. We'll pre-rig and test any stunts and make sure that there's enough safety gear – helmets, life-jackets, whatever is required – in the right place so that when the on-screen team arrives they can start filming as quickly as possible.

During filming, we're responsible for the safety of the cast and the crew whose focus will be on getting the right shot. We belay them – a technique that creates friction to slow or stop the fall of a climber – up and down cliff faces, or short-rope them on steep terrain, so that all they have to think about is getting the footage they need. Depending on the show, and depending on the reputation of the presenter, it will also be our job to make them look like an expert! With the different skill levels of the people involved, and the range of environments we work in, it's important we have an armoury of techniques and equipment that can get the desired results safely in the shortest amount of time.

Many people imagine a lot of money is involved in making TV programmes, but that isn't always the case. And when budgets get tight, so do schedules – we now create the content we used to make over a fortnight in a few days. It's exciting and challenging for the safety crew because we have to think meticulously through all possible scenarios so we can minimise and mitigate the risks involved. Thinking fast and problem-solving is a part of my work that I love.

Everyone on the crew wants to make amazing TV, but it's our job to ensure it gets made safely. Sometimes – after careful consideration – that means saying no to certain stunts, although we'll always come up with an alternative. This is where our expertise lies because we understand, and antic- ipate, when and where potential problems are lurking. Then we can either eliminate them or incorporate them into our planning.

Even though I work with the best team in the business, it doesn't mean any of us can ever switch off and hope someone else has covered all the bases. I was working in Costa Rica on a television show where I had to abseil down a cliff in the middle of the jungle with the presenter and some contestants. I didn't know this at the time, but another member of the safety team had come up with an idea to give the producers some really fun footage. He set up the ropes in such a way that there was an extra loop called a prusik cord in the abseil line. His idea was that the prusik cord could be cut and the contestant – or the presenter, or me – would instantly drop down by the length of the loop and think the rope system had failed. Cue screaming. Cue drama. Cue happy producer.

Thankfully, Stani realised that the cord was about to be cut in the wrong way, with the blade facing towards the loose loop. If the knife wasn't moved out of the way quickly enough, the slack loop would be pulled tight against the blade as soon as the contestant dropped down. When a rope is that heavily loaded it can snap when it comes into contact with something sharp: the contestant would fall and would almost certainly be horrifically injured, if not killed.

When I heard about this, my first thought was that the second rope would save us, but it turned out that there wasn't a second rope. Ideally, you'd use a double rope system. It's not necessary – we've dangled jeeps from helicopters on these ropes, so they're definitely strong enough – but when you can make it safer, especially when you've got inexperienced participants, why wouldn't you? Hardly any viewers would notice and it would still make brilliant TV. We were all so grateful for Stani's vigilance. Not only was it an example of the importance of an active mind, it also highlighted just how important an experienced and capable safety team is.

Worryingly, I'm hearing more and more stories about productions not hiring safety crews. I can think of two explanations for this: either they have worked with a good safety team who made it look so effortless that the service they provided went unnoticed, or they have had a bad experience. When people are new to the safety business, they don't know the difference between guiding clients in the mountains and guiding film crews.

With clients there is usually time to rig ropes and talk people slowly through their use. A film crew's needs are very different: they are not on a holiday, they are there to do a job that means working quickly. The change of pace can come as a bit of a shock, which may lead inexperienced safety teams to put a stop to certain activities because they treat the crew as if they were expedition clients. That means the crew doesn't get the shots they need, and on the next

90

project the producers think they might make better TV if they don't take a safety team.

I was recently working with a medic in South Africa who had just walked off another show precisely because the producers weren't listening to his concerns. He'd been on a production where the safety team had consisted of a single armed ranger. When he questioned this, he was told that a full safety team wouldn't let the crew do what they needed to do to make exciting TV. In this case, 'exciting TV' had meant contestants eating poisonous fruit that resulted in permanent liver and kidney damage. Not only is that immoral, but a professional safety team would have helped the producers get even more exciting footage. We can help crews push boundaries further because we can create epic stunts safely.

On Bear Grylls shows, risk is inherent due to the remoteness of locations and the environments we work in. Safety, however, is taken seriously. On the most recent series of *Mission Survive*, in which Bear – assisted by Scott Heffield and me – took a group of celebrities through some of the toughest places on earth, the contestants were petrified by an abseiling stunt that had been prepared for them. What they failed to realise was that they were in much more danger walking along the path to get to the stunt: if they'd slipped on some loose shale they could have tumbled down the hillside. It's the difference between perceived and actual risk that lets us play safely with the contestants' minds to get good reaction shots. On a relatively gentle slope, they were all letting their attention wander and putting themselves in real danger.

I had another reminder recently of the importance of keeping your mind active, of questioning everything, when I was on a reconnaissance trip for a new Chinese TV show. It was difficult to tell which orders were coming from the production company, and which instructions were from the Chinese authorities. In the end I concluded that they were one and the same. It made the trip incredibly stressful and we were given very little room to do our work as it seemed everything had been decided before we got there. If they wanted us to film in a particular location, it meant we were filming there! At one point, I couldn't argue with them any more and just went along with what they were suggesting. I let a part of my brain switch off and didn't ask where they were taking us. Which turned out to be at an altitude of 4,500 metres above sea level.

Altitude sickness can be extremely debilitating – decreased oxygen can cause fatigue, headaches, nausea and dizziness, sometimes to a degree at which you can hardly move – and it can also be oddly random. You might have climbed Everest last week and been fine, but this week you're on a lower peak and your body can't handle it. Several studies have been done into why and when we suffer from altitude sickness, but as yet there's no way of predicting who will succumb. On that trip it was me.

In hindsight, I should have pushed our handlers to find out what height they were taking me to. But the upside was that the headaches and nausea I suffered were a reminder *always* to ask the right questions, and never, *ever* to switch off so that I maintain ownership of the decisions that affect my life.

7

Empathy

Empathy is having an awareness and understanding of the feelings and emotions of others. It allows us to put ourselves in others' shoes and understand what they are experiencing. Empathy helps us relate to people and build relationships. It is one of the forces that binds societies together.

As it relates to survival, empathy is about more than responding to someone's distress because we can put ourselves into their shoes: it's about extending that insight to the environment and our own bodies. It lets us view the world around us without judgement, and when we have empathy for ourselves, we use previously acquired knowledge of how we respond to difficulties to guide us to make smarter choices.

Empathy undoubtedly shares certain attributes with intuition, but it's much more about our conscious brain at work than our subconscious beavering away in the background. Studies conducted with children who have Asperger's syndrome have developed techniques for building empathy. Although some people have a type of Asperger's thought to involve overactive empathy, the condition is mostly associated with lack of it, and these techniques include encouraging the child to think about another person and describe what they like, or what they do for a living. This enables them to build a meaningful picture of someone who is different from themselves. Many of us do this naturally, but because it's teachable, we can all enhance our powers of empathy by applying a little rigour. The more we practise, the more we're able to call on it when we need it in a crisis.

You might be familiar with Abraham Maslow's hierarchy of needs, a famous piece of research carried out in the 1940s to identify what motivates humans. It's usually depicted as a triangle with five tiers. The bottom layer consists of the basic requirements to sustain life – food, water, warmth: the pure survival layer. Above that are safety and security, because without those we can't attend to the needs of the next tier, which is about bonds and meaningful relationships with others. Someone in an abusive relationship, particularly a child, who doesn't feel secure will struggle to form emotional attachments: Maslow suggested that we could only get to the next tier once we had attained the things in the layers below. The top of the triangle is achieving your potential and attaining fulfilment.

It's not always comfortable to admit, but the way of getting to the top of the triangle is to say 'no' to others and 'yes' to yourself. To be a fully successful human, the theory goes, you have to know yourself properly and that is what having empathy for yourself really means.

Personal empathy is partially about acceptance, but it's also about understanding that you have needs, thoughts and feelings, and that these might differ from those of the people and the environment around you. Recognising them allows you to perform at your best and do what it takes to survive.

The saying 'before you help others you must first help yourself' is very relevant in a survival situation. If you can identify, accept and meet your own needs, or at least know you're working towards getting them met, it goes a long way towards self-preservation. When you're OK, it's much easier to support others than when you're struggling to meet your basic needs. A couple who are separating, for example, might want to come to terms with the reality of divorce before telling their children. The simplest illustration of this is the in-flight safety instruction to put your own oxygen mask on before you help others. You can apply this to other areas of life: once you have put on your metaphorical oxygen mask and can breathe, you are in a better position to help someone else.

The danger with empathy is in allowing the profound feelings we have for other people to spill over into sympathy. If empathy enables us to understand and accept that someone may feel a certain way, or to predict how they are feeling, sympathy is when we take on their emotions. A good – but rather extreme – illustration of this is something called Couvade syndrome, also known as sympathetic pregnancy syndrome: a partner will display some of the same symptoms and behaviours as a pregnant woman, such as weight gain, morning nausea, altered hormone levels and disturbed sleep patterns. In a survival situation, sympathy can be dangerous because it stops you tuning in to your intuition, as well as the signals from the environment around you.

As an expedition leader, it's important I maintain the boundary between empathising with my clients and sympathising with them. I learnt this the hard way on a trip in Mexico. I was taking a group of clients up the Pico de Orizaba, the third highest mountain in the Americas. There was a group of five friends from the US, in their forties and fifties – four men and a woman – plus a local guide. It's a popular mountain for non-mountaineers as it's not a particularly technical climb. The Orizaba is a dormant volcano, so it has quite a gentle profile compared to something like the Matterhorn, but you still need crampons and ice axes to make your way over the glacier. It is an isolated peak, so is prominent in the landscape, which makes it all too easy to focus on one thing: getting to the summit.

We'd taken things fairly gently, spending nights at various camps on the way up, making sure we acclimatised to the altitude. On the final morning we packed up and were preparing to walk to the summit, but something about the weather didn't feel right to me. It was five or six in the morning, the sun had just come up, and I thought the sky looked oddly yellow. I didn't know exactly what was bothering me about it, but it hadn't been that colour on previous mornings. I mentioned it to the local guide, and he agreed it looked ominous.

I called my group together and told them I thought the weather was about to change and that we should stay in the hut. It was a really difficult conversation because all I could tell them was that I had a feeling. Understandably, they wanted evidence – proof, even – that we shouldn't go for the summit. One of my concerns on mountains like the Orizaba is exposure – there's no protection once you get up high: if the weather turned nasty, we could potentially be in a lot of trouble. Of course, what made the conversation harder was that they were paying me to get them to the summit.

'Summit fever' is an overriding irrational need to get to a summit even when you know it's not safe to do so, and even experienced mountaineers can suffer from it. When you've already climbed several thousand metres and the summit is only a few hundred metres away, you can understand why people think getting to the top is within their capabilities. When you've gone that far, and got so close, the idea that you won't make the summit is like having a dream taken away – but when you're several thousand metres up, a few hundred metres is actually a very long way.

My argument wasn't helped when the other group who were using the hut decided to leave and head up. One guy in my party kept asking for proof that a storm was coming, but there was no phone signal up there, so I couldn't pull something up on Google. It didn't help that when they looked out of the window it was sunny and they could actually see the summit.

It was really, really hard not to get sucked into their way of thinking because part of me wanted to go to the summit too. And I always want to give my clients the experience they've paid for. I completely understood why they were frustrated and my empathy for their frustration came close to sympathy with their position. It would have been so easy to say, 'OK, let's go for it', especially as − when I'm not guiding − I always feel the need to push my limits and achieve the goals I've set my mind to. I've had to learn to resist when I'm with clients even though the urge is always bubbling under the surface. When it's just you against five or six people who want to do the opposite thing, it can get pretty lonely. In the end I said to them that I thought we should wait it out for a couple of hours and see how it looked.

Two hours later the clouds had closed in and the summit was no longer visible. Not long after that, the party who had set off first thing arrived back saying it was getting so windy it was dangerous. We ended up staying in that hut for another two days, but we eventually made it to the summit. I look back on that trip now as a lesson in having empathy for the environment, but also on the potential perils of empathy sliding into sympathy for my clients.

I was able to keep those two emotions separate partly because my ability to empathise with my surroundings extends to myself. I've spent enough time on my own in the wild to have a really good understanding of my own reactions, instincts and fears, and this affects the weight I'll give my own judgements.

Many people struggle to develop personal empathy, but it's about mimicking what the successful people around you do, then doing those things in your own way. It's relatively easy to say, 'Oh, So-and-so does that really well so I'll copy it', but it has to work for your personality and your situation before it will become part of your natural embedded toolkit.

Perhaps it would help if I gave an example. When you're in an unfamiliar environment it's obviously difficult to know what's safe to eat, or what you can use to make a shelter or a raft. This is one reason why, when possible, I like to work with local tribespeople because they have this information. If they build their shelters off the ground, I should too. If they use a particular type of trap, it's because it works. There's no way I can instantly replicate their years (or generations) of experience, so I have to adapt their knowledge to my own skills and tools. If I tried to build a shelter that looked exactly like theirs, I'd be demonstrating a lot of empathy for their skills, but not enough for my own. Personal empathy, I suppose, boils down to knowing yourself and developing an adaptive toolkit you can carry into any environment.

I've been lucky enough to work with the best of the best: ex-SAS jungle-warfare specialists, leading survival instructors and top mountain guides, as well as native peoples. From each encounter with them, I took away not only the skills I learnt from them but the drive to find a way that combined these experiences so I could develop my own style of guiding.

Personal empathy is also valuable at home, work or school. You might not be able to copy exactly what a gifted colleague or a brilliant student is doing, but you can adapt what you learn from them and make it work for you. You can practise in other ways too, perhaps by employing some of the techniques therapists use when working with Aspergic children and adapting them to get along better with a difficult co-worker: can you find something about them that you admire, or something interesting that intrigues you and helps you to see them differently?

I always notice when I'm guiding someone with empathetic qualities, and it's especially impressive when I see them in someone young. Many years ago, I was taking a school party on a jungle trip in Laos. Teenagers get embarrassed easily and won't ask questions if they fear looking stupid in front of their friends. So, at the start of an expedition, I will talk to them about going to the toilet – I do this with adults too as it's really important. For me as a leader, to know how somebody's going to the loo is an excellent indicator of their health. There's no point in being polite about it – especially with children – so I talk about shit, and poo, and crap. It's also a really good ice-breaker: if they can talk to me about that, they can talk about anything. As a leader I want my clients to be able to tell me about anything that's worrying them.

If somebody's got diarrhoea or is constipated, it tells me so much about what's going on within their body. Whether they're drinking enough water, whether they've eaten something a bit dodgy or they're having a reaction to something, even if it's heat or stress.

We'd been on that jungle trek for a couple of weeks when a fourteen-year-old girl came up to me and showed the real value of empathy in the wild. She told me her friend hadn't been to the toilet the whole time we'd been on the trip and was now starting to feel unwell. She'd been too embarrassed to say anything.

I went to talk to the girl, who explained that on the first few days of the expedition when we'd been staying in very basic mountain teahouses she'd found the squat toilets pretty grim and just couldn't go.

By the time we'd got away from any civilisation and were into the jungle – whether it was a mental thing or a physical reaction – she still couldn't go to the toilet. I told her we were going to sort it out. I was carrying laxatives, so I gave her some. We managed to source some bananas and I got her to drink loads of water. But nothing happened.

The poor girl was miserable and, of course, by now everyone knew she was constipated. It was horrible for her. If we hadn't been so remote, I would have taken her to hospital, but we were days away from medical help. We just had to keep on with the laxatives and the fruit, and hope that something worked.

It was another five or six days later when we reached a

small town and I took her straight to the local medical centre where they gave her some really strong laxatives. Still nothing happened, and she was in agony. That night we had to take an overnight train to Chiang Mai in Thailand; by this point she was very frightened. I was concerned that something more serious was wrong. Perhaps her gut had twisted, or there was an obstruction, which explained her agony: the laxatives were doing their job, but they just weren't able to deliver the results. When you've got that much faecal matter inside you, it starts poisoning the brain and you become dehydrated: any liquid you drink stays in the gut. Which basically means that people can die of embarrassment.

As soon as we got into the city I took her straight to the hospital where she was examined. It turned out she was so impacted that a nurse had to remove the blockage manually.

I just wish she'd felt able to tell me – that she'd had sufficient personal empathy – earlier in the trip when a regular dose of laxatives would almost certainly have sorted her out. When she was discharged from hospital, she still couldn't go easy on herself: she hadn't done anything wrong, just made a mistake, but she wouldn't give herself any peace.

My overriding memory of that trip was her friend's empathy for her embarrassment. She had no idea just how much danger the girl was in, but she knew she was never going to say anything herself so she spoke up and made sure she got help. It's just possible her actions saved her friend's life. That is why empathy is such a crucial part of the survivor's mindset.

8

Preparation

I recently finished doing a recce with Stani in Norway for a TV show, and realised I had a few days free before I needed to get to my next assignment. He had another expedition to go on, so I decided to have an adventure with Tug, our two-year-old husky, who was with us.

It was a spontaneous decision and my preparation didn't involve much more than buying two (identical) maps. I knew I wasn't too far from Trolltunga, a spectacular rock formation with an almost impossible overhang, and I estimated it would take a week or so to walk there and back. I can read maps like some people read music: I look at the contours on the page and see the landscape in 3D in my head. I worked out a route based on what I knew of the snow conditions in the area in December, and factored in how far I thought I could walk each day, given how close it was to the solstice: there wouldn't be an awful lot of daylight.

I marked my route on both maps and put one in a little backpack Tug was wearing. She also had an avalanche transceiver, so if I had an accident and somebody found her, they could see where I was heading. I didn't know anybody in those parts, and as it was a last-minute thing there was no one to tell. I sent Stani a text and told him where I was starting from and when I expected to get back. That was it. Tug and I set off on our own little adventure, no producer demanding better shots, no clients wanting to know when we'd be making camp, just me and my dog and a vast, icy wilderness. So rare, these days, and so exciting.

Working in TV, I'm very used to making last-minute trips as productions are always being rescheduled, so one of the unexpected skills I've picked up over the years is packing. People waste valuable energy carrying things they never use so I got into the habit, whenever I came back from an adventure, of going through my bag and ditching everything that hadn't been touched. These days, I carry only the essentials and, on this trip, that meant clothes, camping gear and food. My backpack weighed no more than fifteen or sixteen kilograms.

The clothing is almost always the same for this kind of journey. I work with a layering system because when your clothes get damp – either from snow or sweat – they can freeze, and you risk getting hypothermia. A layering system means you can peel layers off, or put them back on, and effectively manage your internal climate control.

I start with merino-wool base layers, leggings and a top, then wear a pair of technical ski pants as an outer layer. When it's really sunny I'll trek in just that, then over the top I'll have a gilet, and a synthetic long-sleeved jacket. When it gets really cold, I'll put on a down jacket. I also carry a Gore-Tex layer for when it gets wet or windy. Gear-wise, I carry my tent, a Therm-a-Rest self-inflating mat, a sleeping-bag and tiny Jetboil stove.

I also pack an extra set of base layers so I can use a wet-and-dry routine. When I'm digging out somewhere to pitch the tent, I'll be sweating. Once I'm inside the tent for the night, I'll change into my dry layers for sleep so that the moisture in my clothes doesn't freeze. It's really, really cold getting changed in those conditions, so I climb straight into my sleeping-bag . . . which is also freezing. But, and this is something not enough people realise, it's really important to get into it wearing as little as possible. Too many people make the mistake of thinking their sleeping-bag warms them up, but actually it's their body that warms the sleeping-bag. Modern sleeping-bags are designed to absorb and retain your body heat, and if you wear too many clothes, you stop them doing their job. There have been so many times when clients have got up in the morning and told me they couldn't sleep because they were so cold, and I know they're about to add that this was in spite of them sleeping in all their clothes.

'Tonight,' I say, 'why don't you try sleeping in just your base layers?'

'But I'll freeze.'

'Just try it.'

They sleep much better the next night.

The other items in my pack were a knife, a compass, a mobile phone, a battery pack, a head torch, a lighter and a fire striker. It was only when I got home from Norway and someone asked me how I'd prepared for the trip that I realised I hadn't. But – and it's a really big but – I also worked out that that was because I had spent my whole life preparing for it.

I had an important wake-up call on the value of preparation on one of my very first winter climbing experiences. I was with a friend in the Lake District and we went out on a Grade II climb, which is relatively gentle. Winter routes are graded for difficulty: I is very simple, little more than a scramble, whereas IV and V are exposed, and the implications of a fall are much more serious.

We started off up a gully and after a while we turned to each other and said, 'This is a bit boring, isn't it? Let's go and do something more exciting.' So we moved out onto the buttress of a cliff face. Of course, we didn't have any ropes with us, because we had only set out to do the easy-ish gully, and for some reason my friend didn't have any gloves. Nevertheless, we set off up the buttress and ended up on a really snowy, icy slab, which we quickly found a little too exciting. We managed to climb up it but there was no way we could go back down. We'd climbed ourselves into a mess and the only way to get out of it without ropes was to keep going up. The cliff was almost vertical, covered with snow and frozen turf that tore away in your hand when you tried to grab it. The ice axes were almost useless.

Below us was a vertical drop, and above us was this huge overhang of windblown snow. We couldn't go down, but we couldn't see a way up either. We found a ledge and stood there, unsure what we were going to do. It was at this point that my mate started to panic. His hands were now so frozen he couldn't hold onto anything very well. 'This is not a good situation,' he said. Massive understatement.

I started traversing around the cliff face, looking for a place where the cornice was smaller in the hope I'd be able to make a hole through it. I found what I was looking for but was incredibly nervous about breaking through: there was a real risk that I would create a crack and send the entire overhang crashing down, taking me with it.

I managed to make a small hole but was too scared to make it any bigger. I pushed myself up through it, forcing the snow into my clothes, getting absolutely soaked and frozen in the process. But I managed it and was finally able to get onto the top of the cliff.

I called out to my mate, guided him towards me, and when he made it up, we literally collapsed to the ground. We were just so incredibly grateful to be alive. However, we were still in real danger: we were at risk of hypothermia, of exposure, and of being so tired that we'd slip and fall. Of course, we were so badly prepared that we didn't have any spare clothing – we'd thought we'd be home by now – or proper night climbing gear. All we had were little LED headlamps. We knew there was no way we'd survive a night on the mountain: we simply had to find a way down.

Luckily, on the other side we found a route through gullies that meant we could walk down, but even then we weren't safe. We were miles from our car, and because it had been snowing so heavily, the roads had been closed. For a long time there were no passing cars we could hitch a ride from but eventually we saw headlights up ahead and went almost weak with relief. It was a police car, and the officer inside saw our headlamps and stopped.

I knew, as I sat and shivered in the back of that police car, if we had died up on that mountain, it would have been because we were utterly unprepared for something to go wrong. We'd planned for the 99 per cent of times when nothing serious happens, not the one per cent. When the police car dropped us off, the officer turned to us and said, 'Don't worry about it. We picked up Chris Bonington last week.' Maybe he said it to make us feel less stupid.

Not only can I pack a bag really quickly these days, but I've noticed my mental preparation for expeditions takes less and less time with each trip. I realised a few years back that in the run-up to departure I was putting expectations on myself, which was unhelpful because an expedition never goes exactly to plan. It's just not possible to envisage exactly what any environment is going to be like, so now I prefer to get there and absorb it. If I'm taking clients out or will be working on a TV show, it's different: I'll prepare by looking at maps, finding out about local vegetation, animals (both to eat and as potential predators), then look at what sort of materials are likely to be available to make traps and build shelters. But when it's just me, it's nice to set off and see if I've got what it takes, improvising as I go along.

When I'm taking relatively inexperienced clients into the wild, I send them guidelines on how to prepare a few months before we leave. As well as a shopping list for camping gear and clothing, I also suggest some exercises they can do to get more supple before they leave. Covering the basics – kit, skills, knowledge, fitness – is vital, but something else will have a much bigger impact on whether you survive than if you've bought a particular brand of sleeping-bag: your ability to think clearly under extreme pressure and make good choices. And the good news is that this is the kind of preparation you can do every day and it doesn't cost a penny: you just have to expose yourself to difficult situations – whether that's giving a presentation, or accepting a leadership role at work – and analyse your responses and reactions.

A natural disaster, or a man-made one, can transform your environment without warning – think of the tourists on the beach before the Boxing Day tsunami, wondering why the tide had gone out. In an emergency like that you're unlikely to be wearing the right gear or carrying survival provisions. The best preparation you can make for such a situation is to test yourself as often as possible so you learn to trust that your body and brain will respond. Perhaps you could take on something in the workplace that gets you out of your comfort zone, or maybe go for a bike ride and see how fast you can pedal. Whatever it is, it's important you put yourself in uncomfortable situations and pay attention to how you feel. What signals does your body send to your brain? How could you have picked up on those signals sooner? How might you have made a better decision? What did you notice but not react to? Analysing your responses at non-life-threatening times will prepare you for those moments when much more is at stake.

Not that it will happen often. Out of the hundreds of expeditions I've been on, I can count the times I've been in fear of my life on one hand. On one such occasion, about six years ago, I was in the jungle in Thailand when I found myself with a gun pointed at me.

I was filming a TV show and had a contestant, a camera operator and a producer with me. The contestant was quite fit, athletic – he was a dancer – and in his twenties, but the two guys on the crew were a little older and a bit out of shape. We were trekking through dense primary jungle, going up and down ridges like knife edges that were four or five hundred feet high. It was really humid, and the most ground we could cover in a day was a couple of kilometres. It looks like nothing on a map, but that's because the maps are made from aerial photography that only captures the height of the jungle canopy. The terrain at ground level was completely different.

It was an extremely physical trek, but we were managing

to keep relatively well hydrated: we'd made water-carriers out of bamboo and rattan and boiled our daily rations every morning. There were also liana vines in the area, which naturally hold and filter water – all you have to do is cut them and you can literally pour the water into your mouth.

On the fifth day, we had been walking for three or four hours when we approached the crest of another ridge. It always feels good getting to the top because you know that, in a few minutes, you'll be walking downhill, but when we got closer to that crest it suddenly opened out into a field. It looked as if it had been cleared by burning and was pretty large, maybe a hundred metres across, and fairly ragged. I immediately knew the waist-high crop was poppies. Opium poppies. There was only a moment to think, Well, this is a bit weird, before I saw the men with rifles.

'Get down!'

The camera guy had been looking through the lens and took a moment to react.

'Get down!'

The armed men had seen us and we could hear them shouting. They were coming towards us.

'We need to get out of here right now,' I said to the team. The contestant was so startled I wasn't sure he'd be able to respond. But he had to: I was in no doubt we would be killed otherwise.

There was a very good reason why I knew our lives were in danger: preparation. Before we'd left for the jungle, I'd had a drink with one of the local fixers the production company used, and he'd mentioned that there were opium groves in the area. Possibly if I hadn't had that conversation, I might not immediately have recognised the crop because the poppies weren't in flower. I also might not have responded quite so decisively, but the fixer had left me in no doubt that the men who guard the opium trade will shoot on sight. The crop is so valuable, and so illegal, they'll kill anyone who might tell the authorities where their fields are. If we had been armed it would have been them or us, but we weren't armed so our only option was to run.

We were already exhausted from the climb but I set off along the ridge, trying not to go straight down because there was a real risk of slipping and falling: if you fell over there you were a sitting target. I also didn't want us to get trapped in the bottom of the valley. Crouching low and forging our way through the undergrowth, we ran as fast as we could. Behind us, the men with rifles were shouting. I tried to put as many trees as possible between us and them, zigzagging to make us harder to hit. I don't remember them firing, but the producer says they did.

The contestant and I were able to keep the pace up, but the cameraman – who was filming on a relatively small Canon – was in danger of lagging behind. He fell a few times and slid in the mud before he was able to get up. I remember becoming hyperaware of the terrain in front of us, almost animalistic, making sure I wasn't leading us into a trap or over a cliff. I could hear the camera guy behind me, his breathing getting heavier. There was a fallen tree trunk up ahead: it was too big to go round, but I wasn't sure he'd be able to climb over it.

I gave him a hand while the other two scrambled over. It gave me a chance to glance back: I couldn't see the gunmen but I could still hear them. We had to keep on running. I could tell the camera guy couldn't take much more.

We'd been running for almost an hour when I thought we might have gone far enough. I started looking for somewhere we could take shelter and spotted a fallen tree surrounded by a load of debris. The four of us crouched behind it and tried to get our breath back. The adrenaline was pumping so hard I couldn't hear if we were still being followed because the blood was pounding in my ears. Every second we were stationary I knew we were potentially putting ourselves in danger. Were we safer if we stayed still, or if we ran? There was no way of knowing.

The jungle was so dense it was hard to see very far at all: I knew the gunmen could just be metres away. They might even walk right past us and not see us. When my pulse softened a little, I started to tune in to the sounds around us, but as I was listening out for the alarm calls of birds, insect noises and the movement of predators, I was aware that those noises wouldn't just give away the gunmen's presence, they would give away ours too.

It was terrifying, but it was clear the camera guy wasn't going anywhere. We had no choice but to sit and wait. It was another hour before we felt it was safe to talk, and even then it was in really hushed voices.

I decided we needed to get out of the area completely. I had a satellite phone with me so I climbed – alone – to the top of the ridge to get a signal, and spoke to the guy who was in charge of safety for the show. He was ex-military and understood the danger. He checked if we wanted them to come in and get us or if we needed medical attention. After a short conversation we agreed the safest thing was for us to make our way to the crew's base camp while they prepared to move filming to another part of the jungle for the rest of the show. That meant we had to make camp: there was no way we could reach them before it got dark.

It was a tough night. The adrenalin never really stopped pumping, but I found it helpful to concentrate on the basics: firewood, water, shelter, food, each ritual a little reminder that life goes on. We sat round the fire that night, knowing none of us would be able to sleep. As I stared at the flames, my thoughts kept drifting back to the conversation I'd had with the fixer, how the day could have ended very differently if we hadn't talked about poppies.

I had another reminder of the value of preparation on a separate jungle expedition in Thailand for a TV show. I was in mountainous, dense forest because we needed somewhere for a helicopter to drop a winch through the canopy. My job was to cut a path through from the base camp to the winch site at an agreed GPS position. I'd set off early in the morning with just a machete, a water bottle, a GPS receiver, a compass, a waterproof jacket and a radio. I'd been climbing uphill and cutting for about eight hours by the time I reached the GPS position, then had to create enough space between the trees for the winch to get through. It was extremely physical work in hot, humid conditions. By the time I'd finished cutting, it was mid-afternoon and I knew there wouldn't be many hours of daylight left to get back to camp. I wasn't worried: there was now a trail I could follow.

However, when I looked around I couldn't see it.

When I make a trail I always leave flash marks on the trunks of trees – basically cutting out a diamond of bark so there are white wood beacons contrasting against the dark bark – but I couldn't see any. So I picked up my GPS receiver knowing all I had to do was reverse the settings and I'd be able to backtrack to my starting point. But the battery had died and I wasn't carrying a spare. I looked again for my cut marks, but I just couldn't spot them.

The jungle was incredibly dense. I was surrounded by hundred-metre tall trees and was completely enclosed. Whichever way I turned, everything looked exactly the same. Visibility in the jungle can be a bit like being in fog: you can really only see a couple of hundred feet because the foliage is so lush and so dense. And under the thick canopy I couldn't see the sun: there was just no way of knowing which way to go.

Suddenly an overwhelming sense of panic rose from my chest. I was hours from base camp, it was late in the day and I wasn't carrying the kind of gear that would make spending a night in the jungle safe and comfortable. It was also extremely hot and I knew I was dehydrated. I could actually feel the panic starting to close down my brain, tunnel vision narrowing what I could see. It's a really horrible feeling, another evolutionary response as your body prepares to run or fight, but in that situation there was nothing to fight and, if I ran, I had no idea which direction to go in.

I took a few deep breaths. I needed to calm my responses and think clearly. I guess it's easier for me to do that than for someone who's never been in that environment before, but it was still a very frightening moment. The more I controlled my breathing, the more I observed my body calming. So much so that, after a couple of minutes, the emotion that surfaced was excitement: I'd realised I was about to experience what a part of me is always hoping for: a proper survival situation. No rescue, no map, no shelter, just me, a machete and the clothes I was standing up in. It was what I had been preparing for throughout my entire career. So I was a little bit disappointed when I noticed a tiny cut on a small tree, indicating the start of the trail. Ultimately, of course, I was pretty relieved.

Part of the reason I was able to calm down fairly quickly is because I have enough faith in my abilities. I knew I could look after myself for a couple of days before it would become life-and-death, but deep breathing is a great way for anyone to stop themselves making a quick and stupid decision. On expeditions with clients, it's amazing how many times I find myself saying, 'Take a deep breath.' For a lot of people, their first instinct in a threatening environment is to do anything, when very often doing nothing for a few minutes will help them make a better choice. I see it all the time. Once clients are confident about fire-lighting, for example, they're keen to get a fire going as quickly as possible, but I often have to stop them. It only takes two or three minutes to light a fire, but it takes two or three hours to prepare to light one. That means gathering enough wood to last the night. It means collecting the water you're going to boil. If you don't prepare properly, you'll run out of fuel, or find the flame went out while you were finding food and water. Preparation can be hard work but, as in any other walk of life, it always pays off in the end.

Running in the Alps, in my happy place

Behind the scenes shot from the show 'Car vs Wild'

Guiding private clients above the ice flows in Patagonia

Hunting and catching scorpions for a TV shoot in Mexico

Megan Hine

Ice climbing near Chamonix in the French Alps

Trekking into basecamp to climb a 6000m peak in the Himalaya with clients.
This valley was sadly hit by the recent landslides in Nepal

Alpine Mountaineering above Courmayeur in Italy

Leading a dog sled and survival expedition in the Arctic

Wild camping while running a winter mountain skills module
for a Dutch University degree course

Teaching jungle survival skills. Using tools such as knifes and machetes in remote places can be dangerous so I always teach knife work early on so it becomes ingrained where your hands are in relation to cutting edges

A remote jungle village, we had been in the jungle in hammocks for 2 weeks, this was the first village we came across, the villagers were so welcoming and put us up in their long house, regaled us with local stories and we spent the night dancing and sampling locally brewed bamboo wines and spirits

It's always difficult filming underground due to the dark. When we do it often involves tight logistics and super lightweight light systems

Guiding in Nepal

9

The Open Mind

When a plane falls out of the sky, it's pure luck as to whether you survive or not. Forces beyond your control will determine if your descent is broken by the canopy of the rainforest or if you're sitting in the part of the fuselage that doesn't break up on impact. And if you do survive the crash and somehow manage to crawl out of the wreckage, luck will still play a huge part in whether or not you make it back to civilisation. Some people – like Juliane Koepcke who survived the plane crash in the Amazon – don't leave things to chance and take action to try to make their way home, while others wait for rescue. There's absolutely no way of knowing which course of action is most likely to lead to survival, but I've long been curious about why we make different choices: why do some people seek out solutions and others just wait? I think it may be because some of us have an open mind that drives us to explore – both emotionally and physically – the environment we find ourselves in.

An open mind has allowed me to have some amazing spiritual experiences, where I've felt the energy of the wilderness flow into my body and surge through my thoughts: it's one of the best reasons I know to spend time in the wild. When you ditch your ego and let yourself become part of something bigger, something universal, you find your awareness of your surroundings expands to allow you to sense possibilities that would otherwise remain just out of reach. It's the kind of hyperawareness that could save your life in a disaster.

The past few years have been incredibly stressful for me. I contracted Lyme disease from a tick in the Lake District, which took a lot out of me physically, emotionally and spiritually. I felt as though the mind-body connection I'd experienced for so much of my career had been severed, and even when I had made a physical recovery, the damage it had done psychologically lingered for a long time. I was beginning to think I might not experience that spiritual connection to the landscape again. Then, a few months ago, I was on a trip to China and we went up into Tibet at an altitude of five thousand metres. I found myself sitting at the edge of a lake with the most incredible view in front of me and felt my mind open up. All the armour around my thoughts simply fell away and the energy of that stunning place was running through my brain and my body: it was simultaneously awesome and humbling. This complete physical, mental and spiritual awareness of being part of something greater than myself made me feel small, but it didn't make me feel insignificant. Incredible experiences like that remind us that individually we are not very important: it's being part of a whole that matters.

When you're in the wild, it's helpful not to see yourself as separate from the environment because the more you can work with it, the more you will see, hear and understand the resources that are right in front of you. Having an open mind helps you experience everything in the present moment, rather than living in the past or worrying about what's next.

In all walks of life, it's just as important to have an open mind about yourself and what you might be capable of. How do you know if you can do something if you've never done it before? It's only through experience and experimentation we discover our strengths, and it's only when we tune into our inner selves that we find out what excites us, scares us or challenges us. It's not hard to see that people who say to themselves, 'I wonder if I can do that,' will do better in a tough environment than those who tell themselves, 'I could never do that.'

I've already talked about acceptance and how important it is to move on quickly from unexpected blows. Once you've accepted your situation, open-mindedness will let you get the most out of wherever you've found yourself. The more we can look around us and say, 'OK, this isn't what I was expecting, but let's see what we can make of it,' the better chance we give ourselves of noticing the people, resources and opportunities that will help us move closer to our intended destination.

An open, flexible mind helps you find what you need in your regular life too. If you think about it, it's pretty rare we feel, career-wise, that we're right where we're supposed to be, doing exactly what we're meant to be doing. Having an open mind about what happens next, or what you'll learn or who you'll meet, greatly decreases the chance that you'll stay stuck somewhere you don't want to be. I do what I do for a living because I didn't plan my career: I was just open to whatever came my way. And now that I'm doing this work, an open mind helps me to do my job well, finding different ways of filming so the producers get what they need while I keep everyone safe. TV work requires a lot of lateral thinking and the willingness to try something new: we're constantly testing our limits.

On private tours where clients' skills and experience are limited, I'm less willing to test their boundaries, and that also requires having an open mind. Early on in my career, I was leading a group in the Himalayan foothills and we came across a landslide. It had been raining heavily and a huge chunk of the hillside had come away, sliding down into a raging river at the bottom of the valley.

As it was one of my first expeditions as a solo leader, I discussed what to do with the Sherpa who was acting as our local guide. He said it would be fine to walk straight across

. . . just so long as we were careful. I couldn't believe it: sections of the landslide were still moving! It was about a hundred metres wide but he was insistent that if we ran across we'd be fine. I really had to put my foot down and tell him there was no way we were doing that.

'There has to be another way around,' I said to him.

He just stood there, shaking his head. It was obvious we couldn't go down – the river was too fierce to contemplate walking through it – so our only options were turning back or going up. For some reason, he wanted to continue on the route we'd planned, even though it had been washed away. It was madness.

Eventually either he or one of the porters went off and found a route above the landslide, but I couldn't get over the risks this guy was willing to take rather than contemplate a fairly simple alteration that didn't put anyone's life in danger. It was a lot of responsibility for me at twenty-two, and I wish I could say things have got better for tour leaders, but I suspect it's not the case. Leaders, who are often younger than most of their clients, have sole responsibility for making huge decisions in places where there's no telephone signal and no one to call in any case. All you've got is your instinct, your training and your experience.

In remote and dangerous places, there are so many factors out of your control that you have to accept things will never go to plan. Flash floods, avalanches, landslides, storms, vehicle breakdowns, illness . . . If you try to imagine what will go wrong it will end up being something unexpected. I was with a group of British schoolchildren in Argentina when we ran into an event to commemorate the Falklands war. Suddenly we risked becoming targets and I found myself monitoring people's body language, analysing the vibes, in case things kicked off.

Occasionally, really serious events disrupt an expedition and there is no way of re-routing so you have to change the focus of your journey. It's rare but it does happen, and changing course, not knowing what we'll stumble across next, becomes part of the experience. Once you let go of the goal, you find that all sorts of possibilities open up. If clients are open to that, we still have an amazing expedition.

In some ways a change of plan can help you appreciate what's around you: you stop seeing what you expected to see and start noticing everything else. Maybe you have more time to talk to local people; maybe you find out more about the culture; or maybe you spend time on your journal or photography. When you're open, you will still get an immense amount out of a trip that doesn't follow the agreed itinerary.

Of course, an open mind doesn't just help you get the most out of an expedition, it helps you get more out of life. A break-up might prompt you to examine what you really want out of a relationship; redundancy might be an opportunity to start your own business. Perhaps, like J. K. Rowling, getting fired will be the catalyst to writing your book!

You find out the real value of an open mind when you are in a genuine life-and-death position. A few years back, I was leading a small group on an Alpine trek and staying at a different hut each night. I'd lived in the Alps for nine years, so it was an environment I knew really well and where I could trust my instincts. One of the things I'm hyperaware of in those conditions is the snow, how it sounds under my feet, how deep it is, how quickly it's been falling: all these things help me understand how likely an avalanche is.

I love snow, and it's a passion I like to share with clients. I'll even dig pits to show them the crystals, which, as well as being beautiful, tell me what's been happening in the area. I'm actually a total snow nerd and I take a little magnifying glass so I can examine the individual layers: it's never a solid white pack. If you've only just arrived in the area, analysing snow profiles as well as talking to locals is a great way of finding out what the weather's been like since the start of the season. The layers tell you, for instance, that there must have been rain, which has frozen over the top of one snow-fall, and then there was more heavy snow because the next layer is so compacted.

An icy layer at the bottom of the pack is very dangerous because water can't get through it. If the snow on top starts to melt, the water reaches the ice and creates a lubricated layer that can make the pack on top of it slide. So, I know that if it's really cold, the chances are everything will be fine. But if it's sunny, and the top of the pack starts melting, then it's potentially going to be dangerous. I try to show my clients these things so they understand my decisions and can make informed decisions for themselves in the future. It's because

I'm a snow nerd that I told my group that day we shouldn't go out.

'But the weather's better,' they said. 'It's not so cold today.'

Another group who had been staying in the same hut had already headed off. I'd told them – a bunch of fit guys in their twenties – about the snow pack and what the dangers were, but they'd said they had a flight to catch and couldn't risk a delay. They were adamant, and as they weren't my clients all I could do was watch them leave. Later in the day, we heard that there had indeed been an avalanche and two of the men with whom we'd shared the hut had died.

Thinking about it now is still chilling, and I often refer back to it when I'm trying to encourage clients to keep an open mind about how an expedition – or even just a day – will turn out. If you can't be flexible, if you won't take account of the conditions, you're putting your life at risk.

The story I tell less often is how I didn't respond to a change in conditions, which cost me very dearly. It was the day I contracted Lyme disease, a debilitating condition that leads to extreme fatigue and makes you feel incredibly low. It's transmitted through tick bites and it can affect your joints, induce migraines, compromise your immune system and even induce heart problems. The biggest cause of death associated with Lyme disease, however, is suicide because it fogs your brain, which stops you thinking clearly. The good news is that the earlier you treat Lyme disease with a course of antibiotics, the less severe your symptoms become.

I'd been working in the Lake District all summer and had

been picking ticks off me successfully for months. At the end of the season, I really wanted a break and went climbing with friends. After taking things relatively easy with clients all summer, I was desperate to push myself. When I noticed a bullseye rash on my right hip I knew I'd been bitten – it's such a distinctive rash – but I didn't realise how serious Lyme disease was and carried on climbing. I needed what the mountain was giving me and I didn't want to turn back.

A few days later, the rash had spread all over my body and I was having migraines that left me curled up in agony. After a while, the pain would subside, and I'd carry on with the climb. It was such a stupid thing to do. I knew what I had and that I should have gone straight to the doctor. Instead I told my friends I'd get it looked at when we got back. Of course, by pushing myself so hard, I probably forced the bacteria into my central nervous system. By the time I finally got a prescription, the course of antibiotics wasn't very effective.

I started to feel terrible, but then the symptoms would subside a little – and roar back to wipe me out. The bacteria have a breeding cycle of about a month, and when they're active you experience huge dips in performance, in mood, everything. The illness was stopping me doing my job and earning money, but the effects were more profound than that. Climbing and outdoor activities are not hobbies to me: they define who I am just as much as they are what I do. They are as necessary to me as breathing; they are not questionable activities and I need them like I need air to breathe. Without them I felt a massive loss of identity.

When I went home to visit family, I saw my old doctor who, by complete coincidence, specialised in tropical medicine. He diagnosed me as having American Lyme disease, the first registered case in the UK. This turned out to be a blessing: it caught the attention of specialists and the Institute of Tropical Diseases. However, because I thought I was getting the disease treated, I went back to work. I was so frustrated at the idea of being sidelined that I pushed myself harder and harder, and kept going until I pretty much collapsed. My joints ached, I had facial paralysis, which was horrendous, and suffered from deep, lingering fatigue. It was the first time in my life I'd ever had anything close to depression. It was horrible.

My doctor had to tell me it could kill me if I didn't rest and stop working. It was incredibly hard for me not to do the things that defined me, which made it even more frustrating when I didn't feel better. I started doing my own research and found a lot of information on US websites. Some of the suggestions sounded a bit far-fetched, but I was willing to try anything because the conventional treatment wasn't working (or perhaps just wasn't working quickly enough for me). One of the things I read was that the Lyme bacteria don't like heat, so on the fourth week when you can feel them breeding, when you're at your absolute worst, taking really hot baths or sitting in a sauna can help suppress them. I also drank a lot of burdock root tea, which is a blood cleanser and may eventually have helped to get rid of the bacteria. But it took months and months for it to go away, and it was probably another couple of years before I had recovered fully.

Of course, what made it worse was that I'd known the minute I'd seen the bullseye rash that I should turn back down the mountain to get medical help. I pride myself on having an open mind, about being up for whatever life throws at me, but on that one occasion I was so blinkered, so set on having a good time with my mates, that I made a really stupid decision. It was a mistake I won't make again.

10

Resilience

'Never give up.'

It's the mantra of most survival books, isn't it? The secret to success is just to keep at it. Whether it's in business or politics or finding fame in the music industry, all you've got to do is keep going. Right?

I'm not so sure that's true, and am fairly certain it's not the case in a genuine survival situation. I can see in certain contexts that attitude will get you what you want: if you're in an endurance race, you know there's a finish line. If you're in a battle, you have to last longer than your opponent. But in a survival situation, who knows where the finish line is? And, no matter what happens, you're never going to outlast nature. Never giving up sounds as if it should be a survivor's

133

characteristic, but actually I think that mindset is all about you, rather than about you within your environment.

The way I see it, if you've got empathy, if you've got intuition, creativity and an open mind that can analyse everything, those things in balance make you resilient. That resilience will in turn lead to endurance, which, I think, is what many people mean when they talk about not quitting. I just don't believe you can decide to quit or not quit because that's not how survival works.

Your body does everything it can to stay alive. In extreme cold it will shut down the blood supply to your extremities; when you deplete your fat stores it will start burning muscle; if you cut yourself, the clotting agents in your blood will stop you bleeding to death; when you get too hot you'll sweat to cool yourself. We've evolved to do everything we can to prolong life. Even if mentally you feel you don't want to carry on, your body will have other ideas.

The danger with saying, 'I'm not giving up,' is that, on its own, it doesn't accomplish very much. It's meaningless. It's when you stop being curious, when you lose your creativity and you shut yourself off to your environment, that you put your life in danger. You can tell me you're not giving up as many times as you like, but you're wasting your breath if you're not tuning into what's around you and asking questions about your surroundings, if you're not testing and trying new things.

People believe not quitting is important because modern life has become so easy for most of us. In the back of our minds, we know someone will probably rescue us. Either our parents will wire us the money or someone will call the emergency services, who will send out a search party. Imagine if you didn't have that kind of support in the background, if there was no one to call. That's what it's like being in the remote wilderness: there just isn't any outside help. No 999. No Phone-a-Friend. You're on your own. And when you're confronted with that reality, you don't have the option of quitting, so you don't.

I found it really interesting a few years ago on *The Island with Bear Grylls*, in which members of the public are stranded on a deserted island for a month to see how they get on. With just a couple of days of survival training, fourteen strangers are left alone with a day's worth of water and a couple of machetes. The point of *The Island* is to discover how ordinary people respond to something that's as close to a shipwreck as you can get. Would they form their own society? Would they allocate defined roles? How would they go about finding food and water?

It has to be one of the toughest reality shows on TV. Every single person who was left on that island was tested and tested again. Bitten by mosquitoes, rained on for days on end and subjected to massive personality clashes while enduring huge amounts of discomfort and deprivation, and that was before you factored in dehydration, hunger and homesickness.

It was easy to spot who was going to do well. They were the playful ones, the ones who wondered what would happen if they explored a different bit of the island or who kept experimenting with different ways of building shelters.

Others, meanwhile, responded completely differently: they quickly felt sorry for themselves and acted like victims. The only way they would survive for a month was if the other people in the group carried them. But on that particular series, the victim culture started to infect the entire group, and at the end of the third week they all gave up. They'd had enough. They wanted to be collected and taken to a nice hotel. They simply sat down and refused to do anything. Some calculated they had only a week left, and that they couldn't starve to death in a week. They decided they'd rather be hungry than look for food.

For a day or two that was all right, but the longer it went on, the more the production team realised they were not going to get the footage they needed to make a TV show. In the end, Bear had to film a short video reminding them of why they were on the island. To their credit, when it was shown to the contestants, they raised their game.

The interesting thing is that I don't think they would have behaved like that in a real survival scenario. The only reason they could down tools and give up was because they knew they were being watched, and there was no way the producers would let them die. Just knowing rescue was possible allowed them to quit. In a real survival situation they couldn't afford to do that because they might starve before help came.

I travel for most of the year and spend time in a huge

range of cultures, and I sometimes wonder how other nationalities would behave if they had their own version of *The Island*. Life in modern Britain is so comfortable that we're in danger of becoming soft. I can't imagine, for instance, Chinese or Russian contestants sitting down and waiting for rescue. In other countries and cultures, people seem much more willing to do whatever it takes to survive. Few of us in the West have lived through a war and all the horror and heartache it must entail, and we've been fortunate enough to live in an era of plenty where the state provides a huge safety net, whether that's free health care or benefits and support if we lose our jobs. The average person in the West won't ever need to fight for a loaf of bread. While we are hugely privileged as a society not to experience extreme hardship, it might explain why we are not developing our resilience. We have been lulled into a false sense of security that 'bad things only happen to other people'.

The old adage 'what doesn't kill you makes you stronger' has a lot of truth in it: the more we are exposed to situations that challenge us and make us fearful, the more we develop the skills and coping mechanisms to face those challenges, thereby reducing our fears. Whenever we do anything for the first time, whether it's jumping off the highest diving board at the pool or giving a presentation, it's massively daunting. But the fifth or sixth time? So long as nothing bad had happened, you probably wouldn't give it a second thought. It's something to keep in mind when you find yourself in a tough spot: tell yourself that if you ever find yourself in the same place again, it won't seem nearly so tough. Think of an entrepreneur cold-calling potential clients and getting the phone slammed down twenty times in a row. With each call she learns something – if only how not to take the rejection personally – and on the twenty-first occasion someone takes her pitch seriously. In the wild, I often talk about claiming your successes: if you've made a shelter, celebrate it; if you've caught a fish, congratulate yourself; and if you've made it through another day you can reassure yourself that it is more likely you'll get through the next. It's a way of consciously building your resilience, but you don't have to be in the wilderness to do it. Every day I bet you could come up with something you learnt, or something you improved on, whether it's your cold-call technique to potential clients or a better cycling route to work. Claiming those successes helps to build your everyday resilience.

Another problem I have with the never-give-up brigade is that we know of a few survival stories where people have made a conscious and deliberate decision to end their lives. We only ever hear of those who make it home, so there's no way of knowing what percentage of people try to take their own lives. This is a topic we can explore by looking in other places for indications of how we might respond when faced with a dire, shortened future. Suicide is still a taboo, and one of the few places where it is fully considered is in fiction. Take *The Road*, Cormac McCarthy's novel, which was made into a haunting film. It's set in a post-apocalyptic world where a man is walking through a desolate, hostile landscape with his son. Through flashbacks, we learn that the boy's mother chose what she saw as the peace of suicide rather than the slow death of starvation in a nuclear winter. How can we possibly know which option we would choose? But I can see that in certain circumstances giving up would seem better than going on.

When there is no end to your suffering is it wrong to choose to end it? I know for some people this is strictly against the teaching of their religion and is highly controversial, but should we not consider the damage we do to other people by insisting they never give up? A few years ago, the husband of a colleague of mine in Switzerland was extremely unwell, and chose to end his life peacefully in one of the clinics there. It was devastating, but it was his choice and prevented him enduring more pain, which spared his family the heartache of watching him suffer.

I think perspectives like this reveal something pertinent about what an extremely resilient mind goes through when death seems certain. There's quite a famous – and incredible – story about a Norwegian soldier in the Second World War who endured an almost unbelievable number of setbacks. Jan Baalsrud was part of a commando unit that was sent to northern Norway to train the Resistance, but his boat was sunk and he had to swim ashore through freezing water. He then had to dodge gunfire as he ran from the beach into the hills wearing only one shoe. Somehow he evaded both capture and hypothermia and spent two months hiding in the Arctic forest. At one point he had to amputate his toes with a penknife to stop gangrene spreading.

Things grew so bleak he thought about taking his life, but was so drained and emaciated he didn't have the energy to clean the rust from his pistol so it would fire. He was eventually helped over the border to Finland by local Sami tribespeople and was then taken to neutral Sweden where he was treated in hospital. When he had recovered and learned to walk again, he returned to Norway and continued his mission.

For him, suicide wasn't an act of giving up: it was strategic so that he couldn't be captured alive and face a worse death in captivity, or be used by the Nazis for political advantage.

Another attempt at suicide I know of also had a strategic element. Mauro Prosperi, an Italian policeman, took part in the Marathon des Sables, a 250-kilometre run over six days through the Moroccan Sahara. Competitors have to carry their tents and supplies with them, but there are regular water stops along the route to prevent dehydration. On the morning of the fourth day, Mauro was in fourth place and feeling good about his prospects for finishing on the podium. Nature had other ideas: later that day there was a sandstorm.

It was a spectacularly severe storm that drove the sand against him with such force he described it as like being hit by bricks. It lasted for eight hours and by the time it had subsided it was dark. He made camp with the idea of getting some rest before making an early start in the morning to catch up on the time he'd lost.

When the sun came up, he found the storm had changed the landscape: nothing was recognisable, but he didn't think he was in trouble. He reasoned that other people were also running the route and he had a map and compass: surely it wouldn't be long before he had company. The map and compass proved of little use to him in a place where the only landmarks were sand and more sand, and after four hours of running in what he thought was the right direction he had to admit he was lost. He still had half a bottle of water and, as a precaution, he peed into his other water bottle, because he knew that the only time you produce urine is when you're reasonably hydrated. If you wait till you're dehydrated to collect it, you simply won't be making any.

The next day, he heard a helicopter and set off a flare. Even though he later described the helicopter as being so close that he could see the colour of the pilot's cap, he wasn't spotted. It was at this point that Mauro started to think he might not survive. But he kept walking, and the following day he spotted a *marabout*, a small Bedouin shrine. He felt sure if he waited there that, even if the organisers didn't locate him, the Bedouin would: presumably someone would come to tend it or worship at it.

The only life he found at the *marabout* was bats, but he was able to capture them, kill them and drink their blood, which was enough to keep him minimally hydrated. He stayed at the shrine for three days before he heard the propellers of a small aircraft. Feeling this was his best hope of being found, he set light to everything he had to attract the pilot's attention. When he wasn't seen, he began to think that he would never be rescued. He decided he had two options: he could wait at the *marabout* to die a slow, agonising death, or he could wander out into the desert until he passed out and hope never to come round.

An indication of just how clearly he was thinking is that he knew how the Italian police pensions worked: if he was found dead, his wife would get an income, but if his body was never found, he would be declared missing and she would have to wait ten years for his pension to pay out. That helped him decide to stay at the *marabout* where he felt sure that someone would find his body. And then he realised he had a third option. He still had his knife. Instead of the lingering death he feared, he decided to take action and slit his wrists.

He passed out, but came round again to find he had barely bled. He was so dehydrated his blood was almost congealed. He had escaped death, and took it as a sign that this wasn't where he was going to die. He started walking again, and remembered a piece of advice a Tuareg nomad had given the contestants before the start of the race: if you get lost, follow the clouds you see in the morning because that's where life is. He took a compass reading of the clouds and walked in their direction, killing lizards and snakes and eating them raw as he went. He started to understand that the desert was somewhere it was possible to live, and began tuning in to the tiniest of clues, spotting excrement that indicated where he might find animals. The animals led him to dry riverbeds where he found succulents he could squeeze and drink from.

On the eighth day after he had left the *marabout*, he found an oasis. He said he lay down and drank – slowly – for a whole day. It was there that he saw a footprint and knew that people weren't far away. The first person who saw him – by now he was skeletal – was a little girl, who was so frightened she ran away. But she ran to her mother, who was camping nearby with other women while their men were at the market in a nearby town. They took him in, and raised the alarm with the military police, who drove him to hospital.

It was only when he was in hospital that Mauro found out he had crossed the border into Algeria and was almost two hundred miles off course! It's one of the greatest survival stories of recent decades, and so much about Mauro's journey is fascinating. For me, the most revealing fact is that when he was contemplating suicide he wasn't giving up: he was making a selfless, rational decision for the benefit of his family.

We can never know how many survival stories end in suicide. When park rangers find bodies at the bottom of cliffs, did their owners fall or jump? Having witnessed how people behave in extreme environments, even when they're hungry, dehydrated, exhausted and demoralised, it's been my experience that they talk only very rarely about ending their lives. People die because they get infections, or they fall, or they succumb to the heat or the cold. It's their bodies that fail, not their minds. And I suspect this is also evolution: as a species, we are all born with the resilient mind of a survivor.

11

The Partitioned Mind

The ability to control your emotions under pressure isn't just vital in survival situations, it's extremely helpful in everyday life too.

When you're in a small group in the wilderness, tensions and tantrums can have serious consequences. Some people like to deal with emotions head on, but I am the opposite. For some reason, I parcel up those potentially consuming feelings, put them into a box and – almost always – leave them there. In a crisis this helps me to take an overview, which enables me to get on with my job. It can help in daily life too.

Getting angry with a driver who cuts you up on the road doesn't do any good, especially as – just like the wilderness

– they won't know or care if you're angry or upset. In the wild, it's potentially catastrophic: the last thing you want to be doing is fuming about something trivial when you need every brain cell working hard to keep you alive.

Some emotions are easier to box up than others. For me, fear and anxiety were never particularly toxic: the emotion that would do me the most harm was self-criticism. I'm not particularly competitive with other people, but I am incredibly hard on myself and have high expectations of what I should be capable of. In the past, when I didn't, or couldn't, live up to those expectations, I would admonish myself for the smallest of mistakes. Now I can pack such emotions away: I sieve out the negative and focus on the positive, which is what really matters.

I know other adventurers who parcel up their emotions, but we all use our mental box differently. Some take it home and unpack it so they can endlessly relive situations or talk them over to the point of exhaustion. Others store them away, then take themselves on a retreat to process their emotions. I work with a lot of ex-military personnel, some of whom suffer from post-traumatic stress disorder after seeing active service, and they don't just put difficult emotions in a box: they go out of their way to make light of even horrific experiences. I don't know if this is something they've learnt in counselling or if it's a coping mechanism they've developed on their own, but laughing at yourself is one way of staying sane.

My technique is different: I don't pack the box for the

return journey. I simply leave the anger, tension or fear where I acquired it. I don't like to dwell on the past. I want to live in the here and now and enjoy the adventure that is the future. Maybe a psychologist will tell me I'm storing up problems for later by not examining the contents of my box, but for the time being it works, and I'll carry on doing it so long as it keeps me alive.

Partitioning my mind and putting unhelpful emotions into a box is something I've always found fairly easy, but with practice it has become second nature. A few years ago, Stani and I were working on a TV show when my mental box probably saved a man's life. As survival shows go, this one was pretty hardcore: we three survival experts each trained two contestants for two weeks, teaching them everything we could so they could survive for a third week alone in the wilderness. We filmed it in some of the world's toughest environments, and contestants arrived on location with no preparation or warning. The show started with them getting a knock at the door and being whisked out of their normal lives, then dropped into our filming loca-tion in the same clothes they had been wearing at home or in the office.

Unlike some of the shows I've worked on for British and American TV, the contestants weren't given packs of supplies and safety gear: all they got was a change of clothes, a machete and a knife. That was it. No bottle of water. No dehydrated rations. Definitely no sleeping-bag or tent.

We were filming in the jungle of northern Thailand

near Chiang Dao and, as jungles go, the area is reasonably benign. There are deadly snakes – pit vipers and tree snakes – but the biggest dangers, apart from the occasional tiger, were mosquitoes, waterborne diseases and human error. Bad planning and not dealing quickly with issues like simple yeast infections kill many more people than tigers.

Stani and the other survival expert on the show, and I flew out to Thailand four or five days before the contestants, but when we checked into our hotel and met up with the production team, we found that the first section of the route hadn't been properly scouted. That sounded an alarm bell about how well the show had been set up, and whether the researchers had done their job or just enjoyed a piss-up in Bangkok. We decided to scout the route ourselves and forfeit our preparation time.

A few days later I was introduced to my contestants, who were both still wearing their office clothes. Anna, a blonde, curvy woman who didn't come across as being particularly fit, seemed nervous and was already questioning why she had applied to be on the show. Personality-wise, she couldn't have been more different from Peter, who was convinced he was about to become the new Bear Grylls, although he was middle-aged and slightly overweight. After a quick introduction, I gave them a change of clothes – the usual jungle gear of quick-dry trousers and a long-sleeved shirt – as well as their knives and machetes. I was carrying a little more than them, but not much: just a medical pack, a map, a GPS unit and a radio. That was it: whatever we needed for the next three weeks we would have to fetch, create or kill ourselves.

We were accompanied by a three-man film crew made up of a cameraman, a sound engineer and a story producer, whose job was to make sure the director, who stayed at the base camp, got enough dramatic footage for a great show. None of them had previous jungle experience and they were not particularly agile, which meant they were just as reliant on me as the contestants. The plan was for the crew to go back to base every night, but the programme had been so badly planned that they often got stuck and had to sleep on the jungle floor with Peter, Anna and me.

The base camp shadowed our position and was moved by local guides every few days. That meant they were usually around three kilometres away, but in a jungle with steep terrain and thick undergrowth we were twenty-four hours from help.

When we made camp on the first night, the priority – as it almost always is – was to light a fire so we could boil water. Water can be deadly. Whether it's bacteria, a virus or protozoa, like giardia, that causes painful cramps and diarrhoea, you won't see the micro-organism that has the potential to make you ill. And when your body is under a huge amount of stress because you haven't eaten, or slept, or if you're dehydrated or hypothermic, it's easy to become extremely ill frighteningly quickly. When you're that weak, if you start losing fluids through vomiting or diarrhoea, it can be fatal. So, even if water looks clean, I never drink it until it's been boiled or treated because you never know what's died in a river, or – frankly – shat in it.

Initially, the contestants were completely reliant on me for everything, especially at the end of the day when they were exhausted, dehydrated, hungry and still acclimatising to the environment. On the first night, I made the sleeping platform, started the fire and got the camp ready, because Anna and Peter were almost incapable of helping me.

A jungle is actually a really good place to stay alive as it provides almost everything you need if you know where to look for it. There isn't a better or more versatile building material than bamboo, and food like heart of palm is easy to find. I also caught a couple of frogs that night, which meant the expedition got off to a relatively good start. My biggest worry at that point was Peter's behaviour. He was so gung-ho that he was throwing himself off rocks, somehow convinced he was both a natural wilderness expert and that I wouldn't let anything bad happen to him.

'Look,' I had to say to him, 'we're genuinely twenty-four hours away from help. You jumping off a cliff might make good TV, but this is not a TV set. This is real. There won't be a TV programme if we have to evacuate you out of here and they can't film any more.'

I had to lay down the law with him and insist he didn't use his knife at night. 'Rescue isn't possible at night,' I told him. 'There's no way we could carry you out in the pitch dark. Even a small cut can be fatal.'

The expression on his face told me he thought he knew better.

I know it's a cliché but it's annoyingly true that, in general, women tend to listen better and more readily accept that they don't automatically understand the environment they're in. They are usually happier to build up their understanding of an unfamiliar arena by asking lots of questions, whereas men like Peter just go at everything hammer and tongs until they hurt themselves, or someone else.

In an environment like that, you have to find a way of getting on with people because tensions and resentments can be deadly. It's part of my job to find a way of forming a bond with the people I'm responsible for. With men like Peter, that sometimes means manipulating the situation so that they get into trouble – at least, that was how I wanted him to feel although I would always make sure, of course, that he wasn't putting himself in real danger – so they are forced to listen to me and respect my decisions. After a few days, Peter started to be less reckless as a little bit of humility kicked in, while Anna discovered she was tougher than she'd thought. It was cool to see her grow and start to become empowered.

There's always a pay-off when you're filming a TV show between making really exciting entertainment and what you would actually do in a real survival scenario. Even something as basic as the number of different sleeping platforms the producer wants me to build can be unrealistic: ideally they'd like a different one every day so they have as many visually interesting options as possible in the edit suite, but we can usually agree that I'll show the contestants how to build three or four different types, which is all they would use in the final, edited show anyway.

More seriously, the producer will want to let things get close to the edge, so we are always walking the line between exciting and dangerous. I get a huge kick out of that, as I have to be constantly hyperaware when I'm working at the edge of what's safe and what's possible.

There's always a choice to be made about when you pull someone back from the brink. When I'm leading an expedition, I want my clients never to be emotionally distressed, but part and parcel of making a TV show is allowing people to experience the full spectrum of emotions so we can make exciting entertainment that's also raw and real. I have had the odd moral twinge about making someone cry, but I've now spent so much time observing people in these environments that I'm generally OK with pushing them over the brink . . . as long as I know we can bring them safely back. My priority on a shoot is always safety, but the more shows of this sort that I make, the more resilient I see people are. In a particular moment they may seem distressed, but as soon as the immediate threat is removed they quickly return to a less frantic state.

Occasionally I worry that, because we've kept participants safe so far, producers believe we'll always be able to do so. There's a belief that, so long as you've got a radio and a helicopter can land nearby, no one is in any real danger.

Those attitudes worry me because something as mundane as getting poked in the eye with a stick can be life-threatening when you're so far from help. On that shoot, I felt the production team were pushing a bit too hard for dramatic footage.

The terrain in that jungle is so steep and the canopy so thick that evacuation can only happen on foot. And when the people carrying out the evacuation are tired, hungry, dehydrated and scared, small problems quickly escalate to become life-and-death situations. It's very flattering that the crew and the contestants think I can handle any set of circumstances, but I never forget there may come a time when I can't. I worry that having someone like me around may stop people thinking for themselves, which means they really are in danger.

During the first two weeks, I would hear bits and pieces of news from the other two teams via the production crew. A contributor from Stani's team quit, closely followed by both contributors from the other survival guide, which is a good indicator of just how tough it is to spend two weeks in the jungle. It will take everything you've got, then demand even more. Peter and Anna didn't know there were now only three contestants left in the show. Or that the plan was for the three of them to be thrown together for the final week.

Having spent so long under the jungle canopy, the producers now needed a contrast and the plan was for us to rendezvous with Stani's remaining contestant at a river where they could get different sorts of footage. This would be the point where – on camera – I'd say to Peter and Anna that I'd taught them everything I could and they were on their own for the final week. Obviously, for safety reasons, we couldn't leave them alone – Stani and I would still shadow them – but we would only intervene if their lives were in danger. The challenge now was for them to use everything they'd learnt and apply it to new situations.

When we met up at the rendezvous point, it was a bit of a shock to see Stani's contestant. Mikael was so thin he was almost skeletal. Stani told me he'd been a champion kick-boxer, who'd come into the jungle looking lean and toned, but he'd had virtually no fat stores so his body had withered dramatically.

I once asked a nutritionist why my body doesn't react in the same way on expeditions. One theory suggests that it has become so used to extremes it has adapted to them. Mikael's body, though, had gone into full-on survival mode and he'd started burning muscle instead of the fat he didn't have.

A couple of local guides were standing next to Stani and his camera team – skinny, smiling men with several teeth missing. They were the river experts. They knew the water well and told us that it was a gentle, half-hour journey to our next destination.

The temperature dropped noticeably at the river's edge. The water ran through a narrow gorge that got direct sun for only a couple of hours a day. Though calm and slow-moving, it was extremely cold, possibly only a degree or two above freezing.

We told the contestants that their next challenge was to make a raft and travel downstream for about half an hour to a place where they would make camp for the night. The three reacted to the challenge with a mixture of apprehension and excitement, but I sensed that after relying on Stani and myself they would find the adjustment to doing things on their own, even thinking for themselves, quite difficult.

Although we hadn't taught them how to build a raft we hoped they'd realise that the process is almost identical to making a sleeping platform: a few poles of bamboo lashed together with vines or roots was all they needed. Not easy, but at this stage of the competition it wasn't beyond them.

While the contestants argued about the best way to make their raft, I noticed a few dead animals floating in the water. I knew there were no predators in the river to worry about, but the dead animals told me the water was potentially toxic. What I also spotted, but the contestants didn't, was a local fisherman who drifted past us. He was standing – like a paddle boarder – on a long thin raft, a perfect demonstration of what to build that was suitable for the local conditions, as well as how to use it. But they didn't notice, and carried on making something far too short. In the end, they made two separate rafts, an indication of just how much they had disagreed over the design.

Stani and I inspected the rafts before we let them leave. It was obvious they wouldn't withstand much but the local guides assured us that the water was calm so we let the three of them head off. We followed in two inflatables: Stani, a local guide and two crew in his boat, the other local guide, two more crew and me in the second. For the next half-hour there shouldn't have been too much for me to do as the camera crew got action shots of the rafts making their way haphazardly downstream. While the local guides steered our boats, I could actually take a moment to look at the view. The gorge was stunningly beautiful, with trees tumbling into the water beneath steep rocks rising above. It wasn't just nice for the director to have a change of scenery, it was nice for us too.

'Come on!' The cameraman was shouting at the guide, who didn't speak English. 'Can't you keep this thing in a straight line?' Every time he thought he was getting a good shot, the guide steered the boat in a circle. The smile on his face told us he thought it was funny, giving the tourists an unnecessary thrill ride.

The pilot of Stani's boat was doing exactly the same thing, and both men clearly thought it was hilarious. It was a bit like being at the fairground, which might have been fun for them but it was a nightmare for filming. The boatman offered me his bottle of water, and as soon as I took hold of it I realised why we were spinning around like waltzers: he was drinking moonshine. No wonder he was smiling so much.

I heard the danger before I saw it. An increase in river noise. A rumble. My heart thumped inside my chest, then I saw it: white water. There was no way on earth the bamboo rafts would make it. Within seconds, both rafts dipped over the first wave and broke apart, sending Anna, Peter and Mikael into the freezing water.

Shit. Shit. Shit.

I shouted to Stani, but the noise of the churning river meant he couldn't hear me. The camera crew were shouting too: this was the best footage they'd got for days and they were really excited. They clearly had no idea how much danger we were all in. I shouted to the boatman, pointed at Anna in the water and told him to aim for her. I don't think he needed to speak English to understand what I meant.

Now Stani and I were both 'eyes on'. When people are in fast-moving water, they frequently disappear from view as they're jostled by the currents. We needed to keep all three in sight as they were dragged further and further from us.

'Come on!' I shouted to the boatman. 'Faster!'

When people don't have much body fat, they sit lower in the water making them even harder to see. Mikael bobbed underneath a dead tree lying across the water. They're called strainers because they let only water through. Animals, and humans, get trapped, pulled against the strainer by the force of the water, unable to rescue themselves.

My chest was bursting with adrenaline. My heart hammered so hard it hurt. But even though my body was experiencing all the usual stress reactions, my mind was incredibly clear: I had already put the anger I could easily have felt towards the drunken boatman, or the production team, into my imaginary box, efficiently parking it out of the way so I could get on with the emergency.

'Where is he?' I shouted to Stani.

'I can't see him.'

Seconds later, Mikael popped up. Anna and Peter were still in sight but they were now thirty metres ahead of us, being carried further and faster than the boat I was in. Then I realised why: the boat was deflating. A puncture repair had been forced loose by the rapids and was now flapping about.

It didn't help that the cameraman was leaning out of the boat, trying to get the best angle. Whether it was the shift in weight or the moonshine, we started spinning again, and the contestants were getting further and further from us. They had been in the water for at least five minutes. They would soon be so cold they'd lose the ability to swim. Another five minutes and hypothermia would start to set in. We had to get to them.

I reached over and grabbed the paddle from the boatman. 'Move.'

He didn't understand, so I pushed him out of the way. 'Sit down.'

The raft training I'd done as a teenager in New Zealand kicked in and, Stani taking control of the other boat, we started gaining on the three contestants.

'This is brilliant,' I heard the cameraman say. I could have screamed at him – he had no idea of the danger they were in – but shouting at that point wouldn't have achieved anything. The more the boat deflated, the slower it moved in the water, but at least now I was steering it in the right direction. We inched closer to Anna and Mikael who were river left; Peter was being dragged downriver right. Stani and

I used hand signals: he would go after Mikael and Anna, we would pick up Peter.

I paddled hard to make progress. Every now and then, Peter would get sucked under and disappear from view for several seconds at a time. I knew he would be exhausted and wouldn't have the strength to haul himself into the boat.

When the water calmed a little I was able to paddle us closer, making up twenty metres or so before we hit another rapid, sucking us through a narrow gap and carrying us forward to within grabbing distance of Peter.

'You can't pull him out,' the cameraman said. 'I need more footage.'

He still didn't get it. 'Look, somebody is going to get killed here!' I shouted, while he carried on filming. 'We have to get them out. They're low on energy, at risk of hypothermia, and pretty soon they're going to be incapable of swimming.' I didn't mention that a head injury was also possible as there was so much debris in the water.

'But you're not supposed to be on camera any more,' the sound man shouted.

'I don't give a shit.'

The sound guy, to his credit, dropped his equipment and started to help, leaning out of the boat, getting ready to grab Peter. I steered as close as I could, but he was still five metres away. I glanced across at the other boat: they were pulling Anna in. Her lips were blue and she was barely responsive. Hypothermia.

I paddled harder, but with the boat deflating it wasn't easy to make up the ground. I knew we would have only one chance at grabbing Peter. If we misjudged it, there were two distinct possibilities: he would become separated from us and there wouldn't be enough time to reach him again before he died; or we would capsize and all end up in the water.

The river slowed again as the gorge widened. It was my best shot at making up the distance so I pushed harder and faster.

'Grab him!' I shouted to the sound guy. With the local guide he leant over the side of the boat. I leant backwards to keep us balanced while the cameraman kept filming.

'I've got him,' the sound guy shouted.

I just prayed he wouldn't let go.

Both men reached down into the water, grabbing and clutching at whatever they could. I tried to keep the boat steady, shouting at the cameraman to keep back: he desperately wanted the shot of Peter being lifted out of the water, but I needed him to balance the boat.

They hauled Peter up and dragged him onboard, immediately making the boat sink lower. If we didn't find somewhere to stop very soon, Peter would be back in the river, along with the rest of us.

Peter's lips were also blue but he was shivering, which was a very good sign. There are several layers of hypothermia, the first of which is mild where people shiver. That's the body trying to generate energy to keep itself warm. Sufferers might become slightly less coordinated, their brain might be sluggish, and if they're conscious they'll tell you they feel cold. But if you don't rewarm them, they can very quickly descend into moderate hypothermia and stop shivering. When that happens, the body won't supply blood to the extremities so that it can keep the core and vital organs going. It also takes blood from the brain, and that's when you start getting cognitive impairment. Once that happens, there is a real risk of descending into a coma.

There was suddenly more shouting from Stani's boat: they had picked up Mikael, and I could tell from the look on Stani's face that he was in a much worse condition than Anna was. We had perhaps only minutes to save his life, and if we couldn't rewarm Peter and Anna, they were in danger of going under too.

It simply wasn't possible to rewarm them in the boat. We didn't have anything dry, and even if we had there was no possibility of keeping them dry. With no equipment, our only hope was to get them out of the water and light a fire. But we were stuck inside a deflating boat on fast-flowing water in a deep gorge. There was nothing I could do for Peter except to keep steering and paddling. The sound guy kept talking to him, keeping him conscious, and I looked out for any possible means of escape.

The gorge narrowed and turned, and when we came out of the bend there was a sandbank. Stani saw it, too, and we both paddled towards it, hauling the boats into a calm eddy, then pulling the three contestants onto the sand. Stani and I didn't need to talk to one another: we both knew what to do. I immediately started gathering firewood and kindling, but I could hear Stani arguing with the film crew: they *still* didn't understand how dangerous things were.

'He will die! Don't you get that?'

Finding firewood was relatively easy. In jungles, rain tends to fall only for a few hours a day, so even if wood is wet on the outside, you can strip it to something that will burn well. The fibres inside bamboo make great kindling and within five minutes or so, I had the fire lit. I made it Peter and Anna's job to find more wood. It kept them moving, warmed them up and distracted them from how close they had both come to dying.

We stripped Mikael and brought him close to the fire. You have to be careful with hypothermia victims because not only do they feel cold to the touch, they can't feel heat (because there's no blood in their extremities), which puts them at risk of burns.

I got Peter and Anna to make a rack out of bamboo, like a clothes-airer, that we stood over the fire to dry Mikael's clothes. Thankfully, the quick-dry fabrics he was wearing really did dry quickly, and within ten minutes or so we had put his shirt back on, got him covered up and waited for him to regain consciousness. By the time it started to get dark, we had all been able to get dry and warm.

The immediate risk of losing someone had passed, but we were still in an extremely dangerous situation. Our biggest problem was the possibility of the river level rising, so I shouted at the river guides to repair the deflated boat.

If we had to evacuate in a hurry, there was no way all eight of us could get into a single four-person boat and survive.

When things had calmed down a bit, Stani and I discussed what to do next. Mikael needed food – we all did – but the priority had to be keeping him warm. As night drew in, we decided our only option was to stay put. We had no idea how far downriver it would be to safety, and we had no faith in the research the crew and local guides had done. All we could do was stay dry and warm until the sun came up.

I thrive in situations like that. It's what I've trained for all my life. I am the classic adrenaline junkie, and the closer things get to the edge, the more I seem to get out of it. The crew and the contestants were shattered, but in some weird way the closer to death I come, the more alive I feel.

At some point that evening, the cameraman and story producer approached me. I don't know if they expected me to be angry with them, but my anger had been discarded into a mental box where it couldn't do anyone any harm.

'Listen,' the camera guy said, 'I realise you needed to step in back there. I'm sorry if I got in the way.'

The story producer looked absolutely shattered and was unusually quiet. It took him a few moments to find the right words. 'I've never been in that situation before,' he said. 'I've never seen anything like it and, well, I didn't know how to react. But I know now why you guys are on the team. It's because you're capable of making decisions like that.'

We knew we'd made the right one, but it was still really nice to hear it from the crew. Hopefully, after that experience, they also started packing a mental box, along with a knife and a map, and have developed the ability to make the right decisions under pressure.

12

Fear

When I was at university, studying for my degree in Outdoor Education, I wrote a dissertation about why people go climbing. I spoke to hundreds of rock-climbers and asked people in online forums about their experiences. While some were doing it for fitness or for the adrenaline, I'd find myself hearing several times a week about the phenomenon that climbers and other athletes call 'flow'. It's when your body and mind are so connected that there's just you and the rock, nothing else.

Back then flow was something I'd experienced a few times, but I discovered that some people were more susceptible to it and could put themselves into that state almost at will. The more I spoke to people about it, the more I found runners, mountain-bikers and all sorts of extreme-sports participants who were also chasing this powerful mind-body connection. It's hard to describe, but it's as if your body is doing something without your brain consciously being involved. I'm more likely to experience it on multi-pitch climbs without ropes, where the risks are immense. Somehow my body moves instinctively and effortlessly, giving me the exhilarating experience of being perfectly adapted to my environment, of being a part of it. It's just me and the rock, and it's the most beautiful, almost spiritual, feeling; a kind of physical enlightenment. I recognised it was part of the reason I took the risks I did: flow was what I was searching for. I was living for those rare moments of literally flowing through the environment, my mind and body completely connected, where the only thing that mattered was being.

But then the bubble bursts and your conscious brain realises the danger you're in and it's like, 'Get me off this rock!' Fear flashes through your body and you freeze. It's absolutely terrifying because now you have to work out consciously where to put your hands and feet while dealing with the knowledge that you're a couple of hundred feet up without a rope. But the fear means you can't think clearly so you're in even more danger.

It's rare for me, these days, to experience crippling fear. Through training and exposure, my mind has learnt to cope with it, usually by placing it in a box. I'm so adapted to extreme environments and fast-moving situations that if I feel it it's often after the danger has passed. It's especially true on expeditions with clients, because if they sense I'm scared, there's a risk of real panic. On one level, humans are pack animals, and if one horse bolts, we all do. I work very hard not to show fear, which means talking calmly and controlling my body language. I think this is similar to what cabin crew are trained to do: whatever announcement comes from the cockpit, their faces never give anything away. Like them, I've learnt to control my response to fear, but I've also learnt that when I do get frightened it's for a very good reason.

There's nothing macho or impressive about not being scared. In fact, if you never feel fear it almost certainly means you're not recognising when you're in trouble: it's an evolutionary response to danger. Fear is an indication that something is wrong and your body is telling you to be aware of it. It is an instinct that can help you fight or make you run. When I feel the twinges of fear, I know I need to look around and discover what the threat is. If it's obvious – like rigging ropes on the edge of a cliff – I'll use logical reasoning to accept the risk and shut the feeling down. I tell myself, 'Yes, I'm high up and this is exposed, but I'm safe. I'm attached by a rope to the rock and it's highly unlikely that this system will fail.' Once the fear has been registered, pinpointed and accepted, it can be put into a box.

Fear is something we also experience in our everyday lives but, unlike when you're hanging on a rope over a cliff edge, it can be hard to pinpoint the exact cause. These less obvious metaphorical cliffs aren't so easily conquered with rational thought and often lead to chronic anxiety. A parent facing redundancy or a building contractor who can't work due to injury may be scared about their ability to pay the mortgage. We experience fear that we'll be overlooked for promotion or left out of social events, which can be toxic. I've found being able to control fear at the cliff edge gives my brain the ability to overcome anxieties on other fronts too: what I learn in the wild often helps me at home. However, there is one thing that, no matter how many times I do it, I still find frightening: riding in helicopters. I recently started to have a recurring dream that I'm in a helicopter. I know exactly where I am, and I know exactly who I'm with. It banks round and keeps going. And as it starts falling I wake up.

As far as I'm concerned, they're just not supposed to be in the air. Too many of them fall out of the sky. And when they do crash there's nothing you can do. You're basically inside a rock. There's little chance of gliding until you find a safe place to land. (I'm told pilots are trained how to glide, but I can't see how that would happen.) If a helicopter's going down, it's going down, and it would be pure luck if I survived the impact. Which is almost certainly why I have such a problem with them: there's just nothing I can do.

Normally I use my fear to analyse threats, but as a passenger in a helicopter, my only option is to control the fear. I'm able to do this in a couple of ways. The first is by breathing deeply. I do a lot of yoga, and at the end of most sessions I always breathe deeply into my stomach. I find that very calming, so I started to do those deep-breathing exercises in helicopters. I think it works a bit like cognitive behavioural therapy in that, when my body breathes that deeply, it takes my mind back to a calm post-yoga state. Recently, though, I was in a helicopter in Romania and the turbulence was so strong we were dropping fifty feet at a time. It was the worst flight I've ever been on and the breathing technique just wasn't working.

Then, all of a sudden, this image popped into my head from when I was small. It was a random memory of a big red rose with water droplets on it. As a little girl I'd thought it was really pretty, and somehow on that flight I smelt a powerful rose scent. I don't know where it came from, or why it surfaced, but it calmed me and brought a smile to my face. Now I try to think of that rose when I'm in a helicopter. Sometimes another image will pop into my head, and that's stroking my dog, Tug. I guess that makes a bit more sense than the rose because stroking a dog is a well-known de-stressing technique. If the rose doesn't work, the thought of Tug will.

Apparently, according to friends, I do something else when I'm scared: I sing! When we're rock-climbing, it's a total giveaway that I'm frightened and I won't even know I'm doing it. It's probably my brain trying – very successfully – to make me focus on something else until the danger is past.

It's important to find your own way to control fear because it might save your life. If you're so scared you can't think clearly, the chances of making the wrong decision increase massively. I've seen several examples over the years of completely rational, capable people losing it at the wrong moment because fear invaded their brain.

A few years ago I was on a skiing holiday with three friends, on the Trient Plateau in Switzerland. They were all competent skiers and had plenty of mountain experience. In the mornings we'd take on Alpine climbing routes, then in the afternoons ski down to the hut where we were staying. On the final afternoon, we decided to ski all the way back into town. The risk of avalanche is greater in the afternoon when the sun has been melting the snow, so the sensible thing was to take the quickest route, which was down a steep 200-metre gully.

The two guys went ahead, leaving my friend Julia and me behind. As soon as I made the first turn, Julia called, 'I can't do this.'

I stopped, turned round and looked at her. Her face told me she was absolutely petrified and she wasn't joking. I climbed back up to be next to her, hoping to reassure her.

'Can I be roped to you?' she asked.

It was such a steep gully and there was nowhere to anchor the rope, so if she fell, I would fall too. I had to tell her that wasn't an option. It was much safer to go down individually, but by now she'd had enough time to fixate on how difficult the gully was, even though we could see the guys making their way down below us.

I had never seen Julia like that before, and it was clear there was no way she would go down the gully. I shouted to the guys that we'd find another route down and they carried on without us.

Julia and I skied over to the next valley, but the sun had been on the slopes for several hours and we both knew that in traversing the valley we could cause the snow to slide. It was obvious that it was not a safe way to get down – and Julia had stopped making sense: she was almost ranting about falling into a crevasse. It was clear she was incapable of making any decisions. If we couldn't find shelter, we would almost certainly die overnight, so I attached her to me on a rope and practically dragged her back up the mountain to another hut. It wasn't insulated, had no stove and was clearly designed for summer use. It was better than nothing.

There's a code in the mountains that you always leave a few supplies behind in shelters and we found a couple of marzipan bars, but that was all. It was too cold to sleep and Julia was almost manic. She had started throwing up. It was a long, tortured night, but when the sun came up I managed to get her out of the hut and we made another attempt to get down to the town. The only routes we could find were really steep passes that Julia would normally have handled with ease, but her panic was becoming dangerous. It was as if she was having a breakdown and I knew there would be no way I could get her down safely.

The only option was to call out the helicopter, which, of course, I always try to avoid. But I made the call and we were taken straight to the hospital in Martigny where Julia was assessed. After we'd both had a rest, I went in to see her. She knew her behaviour had been weird but she said she'd been unable to snap herself out of it. We had a really good chat and it turned out she'd had a lot going on in her life at that point – rough relationship, super-stressful job – and the fear she'd felt at the top of the gully had been like a knife, cutting right to her core and exposing just what a bad state she was in mentally. It brought home to me just how dangerous fear can be and why it's so important we all find our own way of either boxing it up, or bringing it under control.

A few years ago, there was a really interesting survival series on Channel Four and National Geographic called *Alone in the Wild*. It was filmed by a documentary maker called Ed Wardle, who wanted to spend three months alone in a remote part of Canada so he could test the skills he'd learnt on adventure shoots. He wanted to put himself in a real survival situation and see if he could make it. He filmed everything himself, leaving footage at drop-off points for a support team to collect when he had already moved on. For three months, he wouldn't have any contact with humans – unless he encountered a hunter – and was going to have to find and kill all his own food.

It made for really interesting TV, but right from the beginning I could see he was scared, and the thing he was most scared of was bears. He was carrying a rifle and an electric fence to rig up round his hammock every night, but so much of what he talked about to the camera was the possibility of a bear attack.

There are very good reasons to be scared of bears. People tend to think of them as big, lumbering, slow creatures, but they can run at up to sixty kilometres an hour. If one comes charging out of a bush ten metres away, you won't have time to react. It'll be on you before you've got your rifle in position. Another common misconception about bears is that you need only be scared of mothers with their cubs. But I've been doing some research into bear behaviour because I'm planning the solo trip in Alaska. I've found that mothers are reluctant to attack unless they perceive you as an immediate threat to their life or that of their cubs: they can't risk getting killed or injured because that would probably result in their cubs dying. Predatory male bears are the bigger problem: they will stalk people for days, and you'll never hear them because they're as quiet as cats. When they do attack . . . Let's just say it's not a pretty way to go.

Ed Wardle's fear was completely reasonable, but as the weeks went on and he got hungrier and lonelier, he seemed to become increasingly fixated on the possibility of an attack. In the end, he didn't last three months, but not because he was attacked by a bear. The loneliness and the fear got to him and he used a satellite phone and asked to be rescued. It wasn't a huge surprise: an addition to the survival Rule of Three is that without human contact our mental health declines dangerously.

Surviving alone for three months on your own is an unbelievably hard challenge, but the clues that Ed might not last were there in the first episode. When he got off the plane I remember thinking, He's scared. He's not going to make it. So when people ask how they can prepare to survive in the wild, I tell them that a good first step is to find a way to control fear.

You can't not feel it, but it is possible not to give in to it. You can practise visualisation and the accept–register–box method in all sorts of situations. You can use them in everyday life to deal with difficult or complicated emotions (try one when your boss has just dumped a whole load of work on your desk). The other technique I use is distraction: if I can focus on gathering firewood or making a shelter, I find the fear gets pushed to one side, making it much easier to deal with.

There are times, though, when nothing will work. I was filming a TV show in Namibia when I experienced the kind of fear that comes when you realise you've become a potential meal to one of the world's greatest predators. I was taking an ordinary guy, Fabian, out into the desert for three weeks, with just a knife, a medical pack and a radio. Every day a film crew would follow us, and at night they'd make camp nearby so we were always in radio contact in case of emergency. We had a camera with night vision to record anything that happened overnight, or if we wanted to make a diary-style report to camera.

We were ten days into the shoot when we made camp near Brandberg Mountain, a dramatic feature that rises out of the flat desert. Fabian and I gathered an enormous pile of firewood before scraping shallow recesses in the sand to sleep in. I radioed the crew to let them know we were going to sleep but I couldn't get through. They must have gone back to the nearest village for the night, but they should have stationed someone in range who could relay a message in an emergency. I didn't think too much about it: it happens sometimes.

Even though there wasn't a moon that night, the stars were so bright it never got dark. Once your eyes have adapted, it's amazing what you can see in the desert and I simply lay down and looked up at the sky, as the fire flickered beside me, until I fell asleep. I love sleeping next to a fire. When you've not got a sleeping-bag, it's your only means of keeping warm and I find you get into a really cool natural rhythm: every two hours it dies down and the cold wakes you up, then you put more wood on and blow the fire into flame before going back to sleep. It sounds disruptive, but a few days into an expedition it becomes a restful, almost meditative routine.

That night when I woke up the fire was still burning. I instantly knew something was wrong. I don't know how – maybe the insects had stopped – but my subconscious had picked up on something and I had an adrenaline spike, as if someone had jumped out at me. I remember slowly rolling my head to the side and opening my eyes to see a big male lion about fifty metres away.

Oh, shit.

I sat up really slowly and my hand was trembling as I reached out for some of the brushwood we'd collected. I felt my insides constrict violently. But very, very quickly the hot rush of fear left my body and my mind took over. I knew

I had to be ready to react. I looked at the fire and prayed the brush took. It caught fire really easily, so I reached over and woke Fabian up.

It was then that I saw it wasn't just one lion but three – a male and two females – and there was no mistaking that they were interested in us. They were pacing around, occasionally moving a little closer, but the fire was keeping them at bay. I looked at our pile of wood and hoped it would last until the crew turned up at seven o'clock. A fire doesn't need to be big to act as a deterrent. Ours wasn't much bigger than a basketball, and although it was tempting to create a really huge fire to scare them off, it was more important we kept it burning for longer: if we used up all our fuel, that would be it.

Fabian and I didn't talk much. We stood back to back so we always had the lions in our sights as they patrolled around us. We had a really brief chat about what we'd do if they attacked: shout and scream to try to scare them away, with long sticks I had beside the fire to use as torches. We both had short-bladed knives and were prepared to fight for our lives. We knew the knives wouldn't help us against such powerful predators, but neither of us was going to sit and wait to be mauled to death. What we didn't talk about was that there shouldn't have been lions in that part of the desert at that time of year. They should have migrated away, but increasingly climate change is altering habitats and migration patterns.

After an hour or so of watching them watch us, something

really amazing happened: I went into a kind of trance, a childlike state of wonder, and started to think about how beautiful those animals were. I could see their muscles rippling under their coats, glistening in the starlight. The way the shadows seemed to cling to them, the way they moved so powerfully and purposefully: I was entranced. There was something humbling about becoming prey to something else. You realise that humans are pretty pathetic: we're small and insignificant and vulnerable, just a very tiny part of something much, much bigger. I felt myself become one with my surroundings.

When you're faced with such an immediate and terrifying threat, you find that your mind doesn't wander because it can't. You need every part of your mind and body to stay on alert, and somehow it does. I don't think I've ever been more acutely aware of my surroundings than I was when those lions were watching us. The stars, the smells, the sounds: my brain was absorbing and processing everything. It was as if it was operating on a higher plane. I almost want to describe it as an out-of-body experience, but it was more a case of never having been more present in my own body. I could feel every muscle, every injury, in that dreamy hyperawareness where everything was connected.

Incredibly, the acute fear I had experienced when I woke up had turned into an almost transcendental calm, and I now wonder if that was me subconsciously accepting my fate. I knew death was a real possibility that night, and it was almost as if my mind was preparing for it.

What I didn't do was pick up the camera and start filming. I thought about it, but I didn't want my eyes and brain to be focused on anything other than the lions. I suppose I didn't want to film our deaths. Cats play with their food and that stuff goes viral. I didn't want anyone who loved me to live with those images if the camera was left running. If I'm ever killed making a TV show, I'd want the footage destroyed.

Just before dawn, as the eastern horizon was starting to lighten, two of the lions wandered away, but I couldn't tell if they had gone behind a rock, or a bush. I didn't know enough about how lions attack: what if they were moving in for the kill? Was one going to hold our attention while the others attacked from a different direction? I could still see one of the females calmly pacing around us and my heart was tight, like a fist, inside my chest as we watched her staring at us. And then, as if it was what she had been planning all night long, she walked off.

The odd thing was I knew she wouldn't come back. My empathy for our surroundings had definitely tuned into something – insect behaviour, bird movements, I really don't know – that made me sure the threat had passed. It was odd how normal it felt, and in the hour or so before the crew got there, Fabian and I got on with our usual morning routine without really discussing what had happened.

Needless to say, when the crew got there, their first response was 'Why the hell didn't you film it?' And then something really interesting happened. On survival shows there's a rule that if it isn't on camera it didn't happen or people could make anything up. Even though Fabian and I had just been through that amazing experience, it was as though it hadn't happened because we couldn't prove it had. So we just got on with filming, and did the same the next day, and it gradually receded from my thoughts.

It wasn't until several years later when, at the end of an interview, a journalist lobbed in a random question along the lines of 'Have you ever been stalked by a wild animal?' that the night in Namibia came back to me in vivid detail. I now find it fascinating that something so visceral, which had brought me so close to death, could have faded in my mind during the intervening years.

Having analysed it, I think it might be for a couple of reasons. The first is, looking back, I wouldn't do anything differently. I'm not racked with anxiety about having done something wrong or criticising myself for stupidity. And the second is that, for those long hours on that starlit night, I was so perfectly living in the moment, so completely present, that when it was over, it really was over.

13

The Decisive Mind

When I give talks to schools and businesses, one of the questions I get asked most often is: what should you do first in a survival situation? Build a shelter, make a fire or find water? The answer depends on the environment you're in: no two scenarios are ever the same. If I'd just been washed up on a beach and it wasn't raining or super-windy, I'd make a fire first because I know that when I'm wet my immediate risk is hypothermia. But if I've been floating in the ocean for a couple of days before I get washed ashore, the priority would be to find fresh water because I'd be dangerously dehydrated. However, if fresh water isn't a problem but the ground is water-logged and there's only an hour of daylight left, building a sleeping platform and a shelter would be the first thing to do.

Bushcraft courses give you the hard skills to start a fire or build a shelter, but they don't necessarily teach you how to make the right decision under pressure. Increasingly I have teenagers coming on trips with me who almost never make decisions for themselves, and find it difficult to do so. Getting comfortable with making your own choices in non-threatening situations at work or school is how you learn to trust your judgement. Decision-making is a habit, and the more you do it, the more comfortable you become with taking crucial decisions when it really matters. People are often so scared of making the wrong choice that they make none, and that's when they end up in trouble.

In 2016, Ann Rodgers, a seventy-two-year-old from Arizona, drove to visit her grandchildren in another part of the state. At some point, she took a wrong turn and her hybrid car ran out of power on an isolated road. She had her pet cat and dog with her, an atlas and a fair bit of food and water. She could see from the atlas she was in canyon country – not somewhere you venture unprepared – so she decided her best bet was to stay with her pets in the car. When no one passed after two days, she reconsidered her choice and decided to rescue herself. She was running low on supplies and she had to find water.

She left her cat in the car with a window ajar and set off into the wilderness with her dog, Queenie. Ann was a keen hiker and had some really useful items in her car: binoculars, a phone, a penknife, a lighter, some matches, lip balm she used as sunscreen, and a hat.

She decided to hike to high ground and use the binoculars to look for a water source. She saw no signs of water or human habitation. She made camp for the night, lit a fire and huddled up with Queenie for warmth.

The next day she spotted a creek and started hiking downstream. Ann suffered from scoliosis, so walking long distance was hard work but at least she had plenty of water. She also found some edible plants, and on her fourth day she caught a turtle, and killed it with her penknife.

She lit signal fires and used white rocks and elk bones to spell out a large 'HELP' sign on a sandbank, and when she heard a helicopter she signalled using her compact mirror. When none of these things worked, she started to lose hope of ever being found. The following day, Queenie ran off and, without her companion, Ann was feeling desperate.

What she didn't know was that nine days earlier, her car had been found and her cat had been taken to an animal shelter. Meanwhile ground and aerial searches had started and hikers in the area had been asked to look out for her. When one found tracks, the aerial search was reactivated. The hikers then found her HELP sign and a note saying she would continue to walk downstream. The helicopter followed the creek until she was spotted. Ann was taken to hospital, treated for mild exposure and released the same day into the care of her family. The hikers also found Queenie.

It's a great survival story, involving huge amounts of courage and character, as well as plenty of smart decisions. But if Ann had stayed with her car for just one more day, she would have been rescued and spared her ordeal.

In July 2013, Geraldine Largay set off to walk the 2,200-mile Appalachian Trail, a popular and well-used hiking route in the US. Gerry had been hiking and camping in the wild all her life and had decades of experience. She also had a companion, her best friend Jane. Every few days, they arranged to rendezvous with Gerry's husband, George, for a night of comfort in a hotel before getting back on the trail.

When Jane got a call about a family emergency she turned back, but Gerry decided to carry on to the next rendezvous point with George. She discovered she liked hiking on her own more than she expected and, after a night with her husband, she set off to continue the trail without Jane.

Gerry spent the next night at a cabin talking to other hikers. In the morning, she said goodbye and headed off for another day's adventure. At some point, she left the trail to go to the loo and that was when her trouble started. She couldn't find her way back to the trail even though it was well marked with blue and white signs.

It's surprisingly easy to get lost, even if you're just a few metres from a trail. When you're in forests, things can look the same, no matter which direction you face, and if the undergrowth is thick it might be impossible to see a narrow path even if it's nearby. And if that path curves, and you don't retrace your steps precisely, you can easily walk past it and never see it.

Gerry sent a text to George: *In some trouble. Got off trail to go to br. Now lost. Can u call the Mountain Club to c if a trail maintainer can help me? Somewhere north of woods road. XOX*

When the text didn't send, Gerry abandoned the idea of finding the trail and instead headed for higher ground to get a phone signal. When she reached the peak, she still couldn't get a signal, and on her second day off the trail she found a small clearing near a stream where she made camp. She had a tent, a sleeping-bag and a few provisions. Out of hope rather than expectation she sent George another text: *Lost since yesterday. Off trail 3 or 4 miles. Call police for what to do pls. XOX* She tied up a foil blanket between trees to attract attention and waited for rescue.

When Gerry didn't make it to the next rendezvous, George called for help and a huge search, involving dogs and heli-copters, was launched. As the days turned into weeks, Gerry increasingly turned to her notebook to record her ordeal. When she became sure she would never be found, her notes became farewell messages to her family.

Those messages were discovered two years later when a forester stumbled on her camp and found Gerry's skeleton inside her sleeping-bag. The dates in her notebook showed she had lived for at least twenty-six days after getting lost. At times, rescue parties had come within a hundred yards of her camp. Heartbreakingly, she had only been a twen-ty-minute walk from a logging road.

One woman left her car and probably should have stayed put, the other made camp and probably should have carried on walking: did one make a worse decision than the other? In a survival scenario, how can you know which is the right call? I can imagine the awful moment when Gerry couldn't find the trail. She would only have wandered a few feet so she'd have known it couldn't be far. You can almost picture her saying to herself, 'It's got to be here somewhere. You're just being stupid,' and trudging off at speed before realising she must have missed it, turning back in the direction she'd come from, then trying a different angle before getting comprehensively lost. The anger and frustration you feel at being stupid enough to get lost – especially when you're an experienced hiker – can be enough to cloud your judgement. When you're in that kind of state, it's hard to make any decision, let alone a good one.

If that happens, you need to find a way of thinking as clearly as possible. The acronym STOP may help: it stands for Sit down; Think; Observe; Plan. When I teach navigation to teenagers doing a Duke of Edinburgh award, I tell them that if they can't work out where they are on the map, they should get their stoves out and put the kettle on. By the time they're drinking their hot chocolate, they'll have calmed down a bit and be in a much better state to analyse their situation.

You can apply that strategy to any aspect of life when panic gets in the way. If you find yourself running around like a headless chicken, Sit down; Think; Observe; Plan. Slowing the decision-making process can remove the panic that's stopping you making a good choice.

Making decisions slowly has another benefit: it's a bit like doing weight-training for your brain. You're developing your mental fitness so that when you need to make a lightning-fast choice, you've got the experience and facility to select an option and go for it. You can even look at past decisions and analyse why you made them: this will improve your decision-making.

Practising and taking ownership of decisions can help you feel more in control of your destiny. Knowing how your brain works builds confidence and fosters a greater sense of self. You may have heard stories from victims of domestic violence who had no control over their lives. They describe losing not just their autonomy but their identity to their partner because they had no say in how they lived their life. Our choices define us, and the more decisions we make for ourselves, the stronger our personal identity becomes. Or, to look at it another way, every time you make a decision you turn yourself into the lead character in the movie of your life.

Another technique I find useful to experiment with – when my life isn't in danger! – is breaking down a decision into its constituent parts. Normally this is something we do all at once, but if you can analyse each component of a decision, you may reach a better understanding of the choices you make. Seven steps contribute to good decisions, of which the first is understanding that a decision has to be made. For Ann, stuck in her car for two nights, that was clear cut: should she stay or walk?

The second step is gathering information so that you can make the best possible decision. That may include reviewing your food supply, looking at the weather or a map and pulling together as many facts as you can find. That helps with step three: identifying your choices. For Gerry and Ann it wasn't just 'Should I stay or should I go?' it was 'If I go, which direction should I head in?'

Once you have all the information you can lay your hands on, the fourth step is weighing the evidence and working out which of your options makes the most sense. Now you're ready for the fifth: choosing an option. When you've done that, take action – step six.

When their survival is on the line, people usually have the most trouble with steps five and six, choosing and taking action, because the consequences of making the wrong choice are so great. They become mentally paralysed, which is precisely why taking decisions in your everyday life is so important: you're training your mental muscles to be confident and nimble in an emergency.

If you're wondering what the seventh step is, it's backing your decision. Once you've made it, you need to follow through. There's no value, in Ann or Gerry's situation, in constantly backtracking: indecision almost always leaves you in a worse place than a wrong decision.

I now have enough experience to take life-and-death

decisions in a split second, but that wasn't always the case. When I was eighteen, I took a few days off from my job as a rafting instructor and hiked a section of the Te Araroa Trail, a breathtaking route in New Zealand's South Island. It's one of the most beautiful and wild places on earth.

It was winter and there was a lot of snow, which meant the trail wasn't always apparent. I had to rely on a map and compass to be sure I was still in the right place: at that time of year, there aren't many people on the trail and you could go for weeks without seeing another soul. You *really* don't want to get lost.

I'd crossed a few small streams by wading, but then I came to a river, perhaps twenty metres wide, that was waist-deep. I work on the principle that if it's above my knees, I really shouldn't go across it because it can take you off your feet and sweep you downstream. Even if it's below knee-depth, it can still be incredibly powerful and knock you over. I had two choices: to turn around and retrace my steps, or to try to get across. The decision was actually pretty easy – of course I was going to try to get to the other side. That's just who I am. The tricky choice was working out how I was going to do it.

At first, I simply walked up and down for a few hundred metres, looking for wider sections, hoping to find shallower water and, if I was lucky, a sandbar in the middle. I saw a stretch that looked easier but not easy enough. The water was fast-flowing – there must have been some snowmelt further upstream – and I don't consider myself the greatest swimmer. If something went wrong, I would be swept downriver and could be dead within minutes. In all likelihood my body would never be found. I looked behind me and reconsidered heading back the way I'd come. Perhaps there was a completely different route that would add a few days to my trip. But then I looked back at the river and knew I wasn't ready to walk away.

Making a decision for yourself is usually easier than doing it for a group because there isn't anyone to answer to. The flip side is that I would never try to cross a river like that with clients: the decision would have been made in seconds. As I looked at the river I felt what a massive responsibility it is to take a decision that puts your own life in danger. I didn't want to die, and I knew that, if I attempted to cross, death was a real possibility. Had I completely misjudged how dangerous it was? Maybe there was a strong current or a deeper section I couldn't see. I must have spent two or more hours weighing up all the options. No one was making me do it. I could turn around and no one would know I had walked away. But for me, the doubts were drowned by the instinct to test myself and see if I was up to the challenge.

My personality means I want to explore and push limits. I'm just someone who wants to see what happens. I know I regret it when I don't give things a go because I will always want to know if I'd have succeeded. After a couple of hours of indecision, my brain coalesced around a single thought: Fuck it. I knew I hadn't come that far only to come *that* far. I started unlacing my boots.

The natural instinct when you're crossing rivers is to keep your feet dry but that's not realistic. What you can do, though, is get your feet dry again as quickly as possible when you reach the other side. So I have developed a little routine. I take my socks and boots off, remove the inner soles, then put my boots back on. You don't want to cross a river bare-foot because you may tread on something sharp, or you may be so tentative that you're easily unbalanced. So, crossing in your boots gives you confidence, and at least you're keeping your socks and inner soles dry. These days, if I know I'm going to be doing a lot of river crossings and I don't have to carry a lot of other gear, I'll pack a pair of sandals just for the rivers.

I wanted to keep as much of my stuff as dry as possible so I could get warm again quickly, but back then I didn't have the best gear or quick-dry clothing or waterproof bags. I attempted to waterproof my food – pasta, rice, tins of tuna – inside a carrier bag. I put my clothes into another plastic bag and tied it up tightly, hoping no water would get in. I took off my base layers and put them right in the middle of my backpack. Perhaps that would make it more likely they'd stay dry.

Wearing just my outer layers, I stepped into the water. It was absolutely freezing and almost instantly I was waist-deep. I slipped off my rucksack to loosen the straps – that's really important when you're crossing water. A bag will have air trapped inside, which means it floats: if you keep it on your back, it will instantly push your head underwater. If the river is fast-flowing, there's nothing you can do and you'll drown. Some people like to carry their pack over one shoulder, but I think that just unbalances you. Better to loosen the straps: that way the weight is even but you can slip out of it if you have to. Ideally, you should practise getting out of your backpack while you're still on land so you're not trying to figure how to do it while you're being pulled along by a strong current.

A few steps in, the freezing water was up to my chest, so I took off my rucksack and held it in front of me like a float as I swam across. I was washed quite a way diagonally downstream and when I reached the other side, my rucksack was so heavy with water I barely had the strength to lift it. I was shivering violently and thought I might let go, but with effort I managed it. Needless to say, my pasta and rice were ruined, and everything – including my base layers – was soaked.

Looking back now, I can see I made the wrong decision. I should have found another way across, but having made it to the other side the most important thing was getting warm. It was freezing and I was wet: hypothermia was a real possibility if I couldn't dry out. It would become life-threatening within half an hour.

The first thing I did was put up my tent: it was wet but it provided a barrier against the elements. There was no possibility of making fire so I got into my sleeping-bag, which was damp rather than soaked. Thankfully, I couldn't afford a down sleeping-bag and had a synthetic one. It's possible this saved my life. Down sleeping-bags are made from soft goose and duck feathers that join together to create air pockets that you heat with the warmth of your body. When the feathers are wet, they clump together into soggy balls that leave gaps in the insulation, making them useless. Synthetic sleeping-bags have an even layer of insulation that doesn't clump when it's wet so they retain some of their thermal properties. Down sleeping-bags and clothing are better in cold, dry environments, whereas the synthetic versions are the right choice for temperate environments, like the UK and New Zealand.

It's amazing how much you can dry out with just body heat. I had polypropylene base layers, which dried out fairly quickly and, overnight, my body heat was enough to dry my clothes. Everything else froze, which is not a bad thing, because in the morning you simply bash the ice out.

I suppose what I learnt from that experience is that even when you make the wrong choice you can't give up. You've got to commit to the path you're on and follow through. Earlier this year, I was doing a recce for a survival shoot in Romania. I was with Stani and we were looking for locations. The producers wanted as many different-looking terrains as possible in the shortest possible route, and it was our job to find them while assessing things like access and egress for the crew, casevac options, survival challenges, rope stunts or landing a helicopter. We studied the map, found a place that looked as if it would have forest, rocky outcrops and water within a few miles and headed off.

It was spring so it wasn't freezing but at altitude it was

still very cold. We walked for several miles along a ridge, then came to an escarpment that wasn't on the map. It's surprising how often this happens when you're in a remote place, especially in countries where governments have had more pressing economic priorities than cartography. We'd checked Google Earth before we'd left our hotel, but the satellite photos had been taken in summer when foliage had obscured the steep rocky cliff face below us.

We could either retrace our steps, or we could abseil down and find another way off the mountain. We knew that once we had got to the bottom of the cliff there was no way we could climb back up. It was a one-way journey. We chose the abseil option and soon found ourselves in a very narrow gorge. We'd walked less than a hundred yards when we saw bear dung. And it was small, which suggested there hadn't been much food around. After a few more paces, we saw a series of small caves in the rock face, which is the exact sort of place a female bear likes to give birth. It was spring. Cub season.

Normally, the way to diminish the threat from bears is to make some noise because they'll run away. But a mother is never going to leave her cubs. In fact, she's going to protect them, and if she senses a threat, there's a good chance she'll attack. She won't want to put her life in danger, but if she believes you're easy prey, you're at serious risk of being mauled.

Stani and I stood still. We couldn't even talk about our situation because we didn't want to make a sound. It didn't take long to weigh up our options: going back was a trap, and that meant our only choice was to carry on, even though we didn't know how long the gorge was or where it would lead. If we scared a bear, my main worry was it running past us to get away: the gorge was so narrow we might be trampled.

All we could do was walk as quietly and quickly as possible. With each step my heart was in my mouth. I looked at every cave entrance and braced myself for a bear to charge out. The gorge curved slightly so we couldn't see how much further we had to go. It was just one foot in front of the other, carefully but purposefully. People often talk about animals smelling fear. I have no idea if it's true, but it was something that went through my head as we made our way over the rocks and scree under our feet, trying not to slip or fall.

It took about twenty minutes, but eventually the gorge opened out and we were able to scramble into the forest below. On the way back down the mountain, we discussed whether we'd made the wrong choice when we'd decided to abseil down. I actually think we made the best decision based on the facts we had: where we went wrong was in setting off with such a poor map. Once we'd realised we were in trouble, though, we backed ourselves and followed through: if there's one thing more dangerous than a wrong decision in a survival scenario, it's indecision.

14

The Social Mind

One of the reasons that shows like *The Island* – and *Big Brother* or *I'm A Celebrity* for that matter – are popular is because we all like seeing how groups of strangers form communities. Will a leader emerge? Will a feud split the group? Who will play the role of peacemaker? And who will piss everyone off?

Group dynamics is a topic I find endlessly fascinating, which may explain why I've watched a lot of *The Walking Dead* over the past couple of years. If you've not seen it, it's a drama set in the US after the zombie apocalypse and follows a survivor, Rick, a sheriff, seeking out other survivors.

The scriptwriters have imagined several different survivor communities for Rick to interact with – some are criminal gangs, others are really supportive, a few have a dominant leader while others will take decisions collectively. I've found it thought-provoking because it shows how humans might behave after a major disaster. It's certainly made me think about the kinds of people I would hope to be shipwrecked with!

If you ever find yourself in a survival situation, there's a reasonable chance you won't be on your own. Your fellow survivors – and how you get on with them – will have a huge impact on whether or not you make it back to civilisation. In theory, a group should survive much better than an individual, but there are times when group dynamics can be harmful, even dangerous, and that's without the threat of zombies.

In *The Island*, fourteen ordinary people are left alone to film themselves for a month on a Pacific island. If you've watched it, you'll have seen plenty of confrontations between contestants, followed by hastily called council meetings where attempts are made to heal divisions and bury hatchets. I'm not involved in the casting for the programme, but I know the producers think long and hard about who to take on. They obviously need a good mix of ages and backgrounds, and they always have a few contestants with production experience and medical qualifications. But what they're also looking for is a bit of drama. Unlike, say, a long stay on an Antarctic research station, where it's really important there aren't any personality clashes, the producers can't make an entertaining show if the contestants don't rub each

other up the wrong way every now and then. I still think
The Island is a fascinating social experiment because you
never know who you'll be trying to survive with if your
plane goes down (or, indeed, who you'll end up getting
stuck with in an office building for the next few years of
your career).

The men and women who sign up for *The Island* have a
pretty good idea of what they're letting themselves in for
– especially the participants in the second series who had
the huge advantage of watching the first – but the celebrities who sign up for *Mission Survive* know very little about
what lies ahead when they get on the plane. When they
agree to take part, the only thing they're told is the dates of
filming. They may find out closer to departure that they're
being taken to, say, South Africa, but they won't know where-
abouts in South Africa, so they won't be able to anticipate
what sort of environment, altitude or climate they'll be in.

If we make six episodes of *Mission Survive*, each episode
is forty-five minutes and there are twelve contestants; each
participant gets just a few minutes of air time for each week
they spend filming. That means an awful lot happens off
camera. So, viewers may think contestants are being soft
when they're shown having a meltdown but, believe me,
these shows are as tough and testing as anything on TV. I
have a huge amount of respect for everyone who signs up
for them: they are incredibly brave to walk into the unknown
like that. As well as underestimating how much time the
celebrities spend in hostile and challenging places, I'm not

sure viewers understand the extent to which they completely hand over their lives to us. From one minute to the next they have no idea what to expect.

The stress they are under is incredible. They are disoriented, denied contact with their loved ones, hungry, woken at random times for stunts, sleep deprived, and pushed well outside their comfort zone. These are techniques similar to those the military forces use to train and harden their soldiers to become more resilient and to expect the unexpected. A quick way to wear someone down before building them back up is to take away their power and control and submit them to hardship so I guess it's not surprising that contestants can become suggestible during filming, which potentially makes them vulnerable. I have seen some contestants forget that they have the power to make decisions for themselves, which means we have a huge duty of care towards them.

On many of the shows I've worked on where participants face assessment and elimination every few days, I've seen what I'd describe as a mild form of Stockholm syndrome develop where captives become sympathetic towards their captors. Contestants became so reliant on the crew who work closest with them and can come to see the camera team or directors as the enemy. They can form such strong attachments to those that are with them all the time that they become very trusting and open to suggestion.

For example a vegetarian contestant who agreed to come on the show as long as she didn't have to eat meat.

She was provided with dehydrated food packets but they obviously left her feeling hungry. Expedition food is calibrated really carefully to meet explorers' needs – some of those packets have more than a thousand calories in them – but the producers made sure her intake was restricted so she'd be facing the same challenge as the other contestants. It clearly worked: she was so hungry that over the course of a few days she felt coerced into eating a worm, followed by a fish eye. She felt terrible about it and was absolutely distraught when she told me she'd felt she didn't have a choice. She did – she absolutely did – but there is something about the atmosphere on expeditions like that which made her feel she didn't have autonomy over her own diet.

On another series, we had an incident in which a contestant who couldn't swim was asked to jump into a lake. Previously she'd been given buoyancy aids, but on this occasion she felt she couldn't say anything because we'd got to the stage of the expedition where she'd lost the ability to think and stand up for herself. She nearly drowned and had to be rescued.

There are all sorts of pressures involved in making a show like *Mission Survive* that contribute to this phenomenon. For starters, contestants are very sure – particularly given their high profile – we won't let anything bad happen to them, and they can see we have a medic and a safety team. These comforts make them relaxed about going along with whatever is suggested. I imagine some worry about footage airing of them being argumentative, or being criticised by the presenter: they've agreed to take part in the show to present a certain side of themselves to viewers so most want to come across as easy-going and up-for-anything.

I also see this phenomenon on expeditions with clients who may become so reliant on me they stop thinking for themselves. That is potentially dangerous: if something happens to me, they need to be able to get themselves to safety. I try to create an atmosphere in which my clients trust me and feel safe, but if I've missed something I need them to speak up and say they think a rope isn't properly tied or they saw a predator: human error is a risk you can never completely eliminate. It's surprisingly rare that a client will question anything I say, but I don't believe that's because I never make a mistake. I'm good but I'm not infallible.

I always explain decisions to clients as we go along. Even if it's pretty obvious how we'll cross a relatively calm river, I'll still discuss what we'd do if the water was flowing faster or if there were dead animals floating in it. I need them to question everything, stay alert and be aware of their environment so they can retain ownership of their decisions.

It can be even harder to get children to speak up. A few years ago I was working with an organisation that fundraises to take disadvantaged young people on the trip of a lifetime. I was on a month-long expedition with twelve fifteen-to-seventeen-year-olds in South America. We were accompanied by a teacher, who was in charge of their welfare, but whenever I tried to give the youngsters more responsibility, he stepped in and micro-managed everything. When we had about ten days left, I was finally able to persuade him we should hand over the decision-making to them. Most of them had never travelled before and had never been given any kind of responsibility, let alone booking travel and accommodation in a foreign country.

Some were excited about the prospect, but most were really wary. 'Look,' I said to them, 'we've been out here for over three weeks. You know how it works. You need to book a bus, you need to book a hostel and we need to eat. Here's the budget. I'm sure you can find a way to get it all done.'

Because their teacher had done everything for them, this group had become quite lazy and were very quick to blame each other and not take responsibility for their actions. They didn't get off to a great start – it was clear they were overlooking things – but I felt my main job at that point was to stop their teacher stepping back in.

We knew, for example, that they hadn't booked a hostel for the next village, and by that stage of the trip they should have known we needed somewhere to sleep. But it was warm and I figured at worst we'd spend a night under the stars.

When we got to the village, the students realised what they'd done and there was a bit of panic but eventually they found us a disgusting old hostel for the night. In the morning, they called a meeting and we all sat down. I was expecting them to start planning the rest of the trip in more detail, but they actually turned on us and blamed us for not telling them they hadn't booked the accommodation.

The way they saw it, we were the adults, and in their

everyday life, adults are the leaders. But as the conversation went on, they started taking ownership of their decision, and began to talk about how they would manage things from then on.

The next day they booked our bus to our final destination where they were to spend the last few days of the trip having what were billed as 'rest and relaxation days'. If they'd saved enough money, they'd have the chance to do some exciting extras, like white-water rafting. We watched as they bought our tickets . . . and we also watched as they went to bed. We saw that none of them had set an alarm.

Their teacher and I discussed if we should tell them or set an alarm ourselves. The next bus wasn't for three days, which gave us just enough time to catch our flight, so we decided not to tell them.

When they woke too late for the bus, they were upset. They were stuck in a tiny village when they could have been doing something much more exciting, but I like to think they had an amazing life lesson: after that, they started questioning all sorts of things and paying much more attention. It was really cool to see them come together as a team and take control. I reckon they got more out of the last few days than the whole of the first three weeks, which is why it's so important for groups to challenge their leader.

I've noticed that – whether it's on expeditions or in pre-planned situations like *The Island* – groups often go through four distinct phases: forming, storming, norming and performing. They're quite well documented and come from research in the 1960s by a psychologist called Bruce Tuckman.

In the forming stage, when people have just met, you get a lot of small-talk, a lot of politeness as they suss each other out. They are reluctant to step up or talk out of turn in case they look like an idiot or offend someone. 'Forming' appears quite civil, but can be extremely stressful as participants realise they're trapped with people they either don't respect or don't agree with. After a few days, it inevitably leads to 'storming', when tempers flare and everything blows up. During the explosive stage people let off steam and resolve issues, and afterwards they start falling into a fairly settled group of categories, whether that's leader, follower, or occupying some kind of supporting role within the tribe.

The group then settles into 'norming', or the normalisation phase, where they get used to their assigned roles, which in turn becomes the 'performing' phase when they start to gain confidence in those roles and the group as a whole starts performing better.

But then, inevitably, for one reason or another – usually because someone is stuck in a role they're not naturally suited to, or the leader starts to make bad decisions – they cycle back to the storming stage, and out of that a new hierarchy forms and everyone settles into different roles. It's fascinating to watch, and also remarkable how often it happens.

I've talked before about assessing clients when I meet them at the airport, and it's usually pretty obvious when you encounter a want-to-be alpha male, who seeks constant acknowledgement and feels a need to occupy the dominant position in the group. I've had a lot of experience in dealing with these characters, they're rarely a problem for long because I've found ways to assert my leadership, and manage them. Usually through emotional support, giving them a role and making them feel needed, all of which helps calm their ego and shows they are being recognised and listened to. We all need to feel respected, those who are happy with themselves do not require so much external feedback whereas those who are struggling emotionally or feel insecure require more support to make them feel like part of a group. Finding a way as a leader to make all of your team feel at ease and respected is necessary to be able to maintain control in an emergency. Ultimately, I'm responsible for everyone's safety on my expeditions – no matter how they treat me or whether underneath I like them – so a good leader has to be able to deal with potential trouble-makers before they become trouble.

When I was still in my early twenties, I taught off-road driving in the Lake District. Most of our clients were men on team-building days or stag weekends, often they took one look at me in the passenger seat and thought there was nothing I could teach them. I would be lying if I said I had never resorted to flattery and flirting to get the job done but they are not tools I like to resort to. I want people to do the job I am asking them to do because they respect me and will take pride in doing it, not because it is sexually or hormonally fuelled by an implied suggestion. I have also learnt to shut down sexuality and femininity at times when working with men from some cultures and backgrounds. These traits in some circumstances make me vulnerable or put me instantly far below them. I do find it tough in theses situations at times because I see my male colleagues dealing with issues by laughing with the locals whereas I don't have that luxury. I feel at times I have to be coldhearted which is not my natural state.

There's clearly something about being behind the wheel of a beefed-up vehicle that turns some men into such a badass they feel invincible! On several occasions, guys, quite understandably, would revert to little-boy-with-a-new-toy mode and I realised very quickly that excitement was his ruling emotion: it didn't matter what I said, he never heard a word. When you have several tonnes of vehicle under your control on technical terrain, *and* you're travelling in convoy, this can be extremely dangerous: I had to find a way to make him listen, so I did.

One of the first obstacles I took him over was a steep, muddy track through a ravine where the rock was level with the roof of the Land Rover Defender or Land Cruiser he was driving. The track was heavily rutted and there was a big boulder in the middle: if you took the wrong line you'd either end up with the vehicle wedged on the roll cage leaning sideways at a sharp angle, or stuck like a seesaw balancing on the boulder.

The mistake people make with off-road driving is thinking they need speed to clear obstacles. Occasionally you do, but what you really need is control, precision, balance and the ability to know exactly where your wheels are positioned in relation to the ground. This may sound obvious, but when you have the long nose of a Defender in front of you, it's hard to gauge where the wheels are.

Inevitably the guy drove at the obstacle too fast, got wedged and ended up rocking back and forth on the boulder. He revved and revved and revved, but when he finally accepted he wasn't going anywhere I took mild satisfaction at very calmly talking him through the manoeuvre to dislodge the vehicle. After that he totally listened to me. And there were others like him. (Interestingly I found women usually made better drivers in these situations because from the start they accepted that they were trying to acquire a new skill and the logical way to do that was by listening to the instructor.)

It's unsurprisingly frustrating that I sometimes have to prove myself in a way a man wouldn't, but I sometimes think I get an easier ride with macho men than a male leader does. Stani frequently has other men treat him like a rival stag in mating season. He doesn't feel physical intimidation but it must be incredibly frustrating and energy consuming when he's trying to do a job, constantly butting heads. In contrast, my femininity can be more manipulative in my leadership, for example coming up with ways for the guy to feel that what I would like him to do was his idea all along whereas for Stani to do this in some situations would be the giving over of power. I am fitter than most people I encounter, and have lots of skills and knowledge, but there are still times when I feel vulnerable on the basis of my sex. In the past I've had clients become fixated with me – I even had to take out a restraining order against one man after he sent me hundreds of emails over a number of years that got more and more sexually explicit and threatening; every time I blocked his IP address he'd find a way around it so I had to involve the police. I now try to vet people before they come on one of my trips.

It's not a pleasant thing to consider, but if something went wrong on an expedition and I was stuck somewhere for an extended period with a group of men, I think I would worry about the risk of sexual assault. I'm sure we'd like to think everyone would always behave honourably, especially after a disaster, but plenty of evidence shows humans will take advantage if they do not fear the consequences. Think of the reports of rape inside the sports stadium where victims of Hurricane Katrina were seeking shelter: civilisation can break down rapidly.

I'm not often fearful, but on a recent trip to Morocco, setting up a shoot for a TV show, I found myself in a position I'll make sure I'm never in again. The show was recreating a famous desert-survival story, but as we were filming at a different time of year from the event we were staging, I had to go along the route and find locations for the crew to position prickly-pear cacti, which was a crucial device in the story. It wasn't technical, so I didn't need anyone else from the production team with me, and that meant I was working alone with the local crew who were all male. It was a fairly rural part of Morocco, but somewhere that's used regularly for filming, so I thought they would be used to working with a woman.

We were in a canyon that had been an ancient trade route. You could easily understand why: in a country where the temperature often reaches 45° centigrade, walking through the shade at the bottom of a narrow gorge makes a lot of sense, which is why it's still in use today.

I always try to be very respectful of local cultures, and made sure I was fully covered – long-sleeved shirt, full-length trousers, with my hair tucked up inside a hat – and I am always polite and friendly with my hosts. But in that part of Morocco, the women wear full burqas. It is the custom for them to walk behind their husbands, and for men to have multiple wives.

I felt trapped in that canyon. It was claustrophobic and the way the men were leering at me was genuinely frightening. I accept that I was in their culture, and it wasn't my place to question their attitudes, but it made it hard for me to do my job.

There was a local crew working up above, and they kept kicking rocks down into the canyon. It was a hundred-foot drop: if one landed on your head it could kill you. I called up and asked them to be more careful, but the rocks kept coming and in the end I had to shout at them: my priority was the safety of my team who were being put at extreme risk, which took precedence over being culturally sensitive. The next day, the guy I'd shouted at didn't come into work. The impression I got was it had been too humiliating to have been shouted at by a woman.

The fact that I had, apparently, embarrassed that guy turned the atmosphere quite sinister and I felt even more intimidated. The way they stared at me, the way they were following me around, felt horrible and oppressive. I was keen not to get myself into any corner that I couldn't back out of. Even though I consider myself pretty agile over that terrain, there were so many of them, and the only people I could call on for help were a couple of hours' drive away.

I wasn't just fearful of sexual assault, I was honestly scared for my life. If they wanted to take revenge on me for humiliating their friend, no witnesses would come forward and maybe the police wouldn't even investigate my disappearance. I think it was only the prospect that the production company wouldn't pay them – and, relative to what they could earn doing anything else, their wages were high – that prevented them doing me harm. If I had been in Morocco on my own, without colleagues in the country, I don't want to think about what could have happened.

That's not to say I never have problems with women on my expeditions, far from it. While I don't think I've ever felt a female client was putting my life in danger, some of the most intractable personality clashes I've witnessed on trips haven't been between alpha males but between women.

I worked for a while as a guide for an American company and took a party of twelve people on a hiking holiday in the Dolomites. These group holidays often attract single women, and – without wanting to generalise – they tend to be career women who may have missed out on relationships and families, which seems to reinforce how important their professional standing is to their sense of self. In their work lives, I get the impression they are used to being the only woman in the room, certainly the only woman of authority, and you can tell they find taking instruction from a younger woman difficult.

On that particular trip I had two high-achieving career women who took lots of group holidays, which are not cheap – several thousand dollars – and I'm always aware that, while there are clients who take a few holidays each year, there's always someone in the party for whom it will be the trip of a lifetime. Right from the start of that expedition, the two women were hugely competitive with each other, and to a lesser extent with me. They were at each other almost from the moment we left the airport, and dominated the group with stories about how important and successful they were.

Their behaviour was divisive and they managed to separate the group into two tribes. It didn't take long for the bullying on both sides to get nasty. I couldn't believe it: they had all crossed the Atlantic to be there, we were in an amazing landscape, and all they cared about was scoring points off each other! It wasn't a massively technical trip – more walking than climbing – but we were still in a harsh environment where small accidents could become major incidents: I needed them to pay attention because on some of the trickier passes they had to be able to work as a team.

Usually when groups fracture like that, someone will try

to act as peacemaker. People who cast themselves in that role are often very emotional and become caught in a weird game of ping-pong between the factions that they aren't equipped to handle. Often they end up making the situation worse.

I spoke to the women individually and told them they were creating a difficult atmosphere for everyone. When their behaviour didn't change, I had to sit them down together and tell them off as if they were children. It was awful. I'd called the organisation I was working for and asked if I had the authority to remove them from the trip and, thankfully, they said yes. I threatened to send the women home because their feud was threatening the safety of the group. It was – just – enough to get them to behave, but that was one trip when we were all very glad to get back to the airport.

On that tour, we were staying in huts and hostels, but on trips when we're camping in the wilderness, I have a secret weapon for helping people to get along and form bonds: the camp fire.

We've been making fire for thousands of years. It's basically shaped our psyche and it's one of the things that makes us different from other animals. Our ability to manipulate fire gives us purified water, it enables us to eat different foods, it lets us forge tools and deter predators, as well as giving us heat and light. It's no wonder we all respond to a camp fire, no matter who we're with or how tough the day has been.

It taps into something deep within us. Sitting around a fire somehow makes you feel part of a community, and these days – now everything we do is so segregated and we're so individualistic – we find the experience of sharing a fire emotional. People often book themselves on big trips after life-changing events, and that can mean they're carrying a lot of emotional baggage; a camp fire helps them to unpack it.

I've seen it too many times with too many people for it to be coincidence, and some of the conversations I've had around camp fires have been incredibly intimate: if you had them in any other circumstance people would think you were insane, sharing so much with virtual strangers. Whether people are discussing the amazing things they've seen that day, or their blisters and injuries, or they're simply nourishing their souls and discovering new insights about themselves, powerful bonds form on expeditions.

Sometimes the conversations are so personal, and so profound, it's almost as if we're tapping into something ancestral, or universal, and I suppose when you're with a group of people you may never see again, you may all become confessional. If you truly were in a life-or-death situation, I imagine those conversations would be even more intense, more emotional.

In Stone Age communities, when starting a fire and keeping it alight was so central to staying alive, each tribe would have had just one. To shun someone from the fire was to deny them food, or protection, so people who would not necessarily have got along spent the hours of darkness together to survive: a camp fire has always made us bury our differences. Our ancestors entertained and educated each other with stories and songs, and we still have that response to fire: it makes us want to share something of ourselves. There is something magical about fire, which is why everyone is always ecstatic when they make their first.

Fire is so important that I always carry two methods of starting one. I take a fire striker, and usually a lighter. On jobs where I require a primitive method as well my choice is the bow drill, because it's more effective in damp conditions than a hand drill. They work in a similar way – by rubbing a pointed stick into a groove in another piece of wood to create friction – but you can get many more rotations with a bow drill, which means you dry the wood more quickly and create more heat. Throughout the day, I make the most of every opportunity to gather kindling, and in damp places like the UK you should do this several hours before you try to light the fire so it can dry out. I carry a dry pouch that I fill with bark, dead seed heads, dry grass and whatever else I come across. If it's wet, I'll seek out birch bark, which lights quite well in damp conditions.

Unless I'm teaching bushcraft – and, actually, even then – I'll also pack a couple of fire-lighters. It's quite funny how often people ask me how I light a fire and I tell them, 'With a fire-lighter and a match, like everyone else.' I can make a bow drill from scratch if I have to, but it's far better to carry a few things with you that won't just save time and effort but may also save your life. If you're caught out overnight, a fire-lighter in your bag pretty much guarantees you'll be able to make a signal fire to attract attention, or a camp fire that will keep you safe: there's no shame in making fire the modern way.

And when you have a group of tired, hungry, irritable clients, who are getting on each other's nerves, a quick fire is what everyone needs. The sooner I can get one going, the sooner people start chatting and bonding, and we become a tribe for the night. Fire doesn't just forge metal, it forges friendships too.

15

Leadership

I've been lucky enough to work with some of the most experienced and talented professionals in the outdoor industry, and it's really obvious to me that some people are effortless, natural leaders whom the rest of us want to follow. It's also pretty clear there are others who *think* they're great leaders, and it's made me consider the difference good leadership makes.

I know I've already talked about *The Walking Dead*, the US TV series set after the zombie apocalypse, but I'm going to mention it again because I think it tells us more about leadership than half the books in the business section of the library. The main character, Rick, is walking through the American south looking for his family, not sure whether they're alive or dead. When he finds them, he quickly becomes the leader of their group of survivors.

Rick doesn't want to be a leader, but people keep looking to him for leadership so he starts to fulfil that role. Watching, I was reminded of Dr Siebert's work on resilience, particularly his finding that the people who make the best survivors are happy in the background but have the capacity to step forward if they're needed. Rick has certain qualities – he's calm, he's wise, he's fair – that mean the other members of the tribe trust him. And I guess that's what we want from our leaders: we want to know that they'll stick around (that they're survivors) and we want to be able to trust them to make decisions for us. So how do leaders gain our trust?

I've worked with people who seem to think one way is to dupe you into it. I call them Fluffers. We all know one: they're the big talkers, the tellers of tall tales, the people who verbally dominate the room or the camp fire. They're the kind of people you will never, ever out-story as they won't let the truth get in the way of a good anecdote. At first, they can seem impressive – they certainly believe their own hype – but they can be frustrating to work with because Fluffers have another quality: they're very good at telling those in power what they want to hear (hence the Fluffer name), which is why they so often end up in leadership positions. On closer scrutiny, their actual skills rarely correlate with their stories.

Initially, Fluffers are the kind of people groups turn to for leadership because they look the part, and because I think, as humans, we're often attracted to strength. But it doesn't take long for their bubble to burst and for Fluffers to be replaced by someone the group has learned they can rely on. Of course, you don't just find Fluffers in the adventure business: they exert far too much power in all kinds of organisations, probably because they're really impressive in interviews.

I've also worked with a few leaders who believe the way to persuade you to trust them is to tell you that you must trust them! The Dictators often have little emotional connection with their team yet no problem with barking orders and expecting to be unquestioningly followed. They struggle to see other people's points of view and are rigid and inflexible, which can be dangerous.

Next on my list of undesirable leadership styles is Too Cool for School. They let their expensive clothing and flashy cars tell you they're the person in charge. They often give their team far too much freedom and don't set boundaries, probably because they're too busy either preening themselves or trying to sleep with one of their clients (which doesn't create a cohesive atmosphere: keep it in your pants till the job is over).

Occasionally, if you're particularly unlucky, you'll find yourself on an expedition led by a Flapper. They're the person who, when a deadline is due, runs round in circles covering the same ground over and over while hustling their team to hurry up. The Flapper has been known to stress out an entire team at the most inopportune moments and, as humans are herd animals, their panic can be contagious. Which means they're potentially dangerous. Another distinguishing feature of the Flapper is a desire to micro-manage everything.

So who would you want leading your expedition (or your ragtag band of survivors against the zombies)? Ideally you'll get the Natural, the kind of person who effortlessly steps in when they're needed. They have enough confidence in themselves and their team to give them the freedom to do their jobs, but also the authority to rein them in when required. The Natural is outwardly calm and encourages communication and creativity. Like Rick in *The Walking Dead*, everyone responds to their natural authority.

I didn't set out to be a leader, but guiding was a way of spending time outdoors and exploring the wild without going completely broke. Over the years, I've been lucky enough to work with some of the most talented people in the adventure business and they've taught me how to bring out the best in my teams. The thing I learnt early on is that leadership isn't something you can fake in the wilderness, and it's especially true on month-long expeditions when you're with people day in, day out and sleeping in the next hammock. Real leadership has to be authentic.

For me, leadership isn't about being listened to, it's about nurturing and encouraging people to do their best and experience the most. I'm constantly monitoring everyone's body language and observing the interactions within the group to see who's demoralised or shutting themselves off. I make a point of highlighting things about our environment that will inspire them, especially if it's something that could save their lives if anything happened to me.

I was first asked to take a group out when I was working in New Zealand in my gap year. It was just a day hike, and the guy running the outdoor centre simply said, 'Off you go', so I did. Then some of the children started asking questions, which made me want to learn more so I could tell them more. I discovered that guiding was a way of sharing my knowledge and enthusiasm, and when I had clients who didn't seem to care, I enjoyed the challenge of engaging them. I still do: I want everyone who comes out with me to be as amazed and awed by the natural world as I am. If they aren't, I've failed at my job.

When I came back to the UK, I trained to be a mountain leader, and when I got my certificate I was told I was one of the youngest people in the country to qualify. Although the training was an eighteenth-birthday present from my parents, I remember putting it off for a while because I didn't want to fail. If I hadn't qualified, it wouldn't have been like failing an ordinary exam: it would almost have meant I'd failed at being me. When I started taking people on expeditions, I was occasionally confronted with the fact that I did not meet their expectations of what a leader looked like: I was too young and too female.

Britain might indeed have its second female prime minister, but there are certain professions in which the ratio of men to women is overwhelming, and the adventure industry is one of them. I'm so used to being the only woman on an expedition – this goes right back to when I was in the cadets at school – that I don't think about it that much. But every now and then someone will say something to me in a manner that I don't hear them using with my male colleagues. I noticed it particularly when I was running bushcraft courses: plenty of men came on those trips with the idea they were about to experience some kind of caveman Utopia and were clearly confused that a woman could either enjoy or be good at it. (Of course, the irony is that most bushcraft skills would traditionally have been used by women because the men would have been hunting.) I got the impression that for some my presence was somehow undermining their manliness. I still feel this with some of the guys I work with in TV: I don't think it's sexism, just lack of exposure to women in these roles – they soon embrace the idea though which is why I am an advocate for showing and doing rather than jumping up and down and making a song and dance about it. People need time to adapt to new concepts and ideas.

I didn't have any female role models in the business when I first started out and there still aren't very many of us at the top levels in it, so this obviously affects how newcomers imagine their leaders will look. I didn't set out to be a role model, but I'm very happy that the next generation can see me and, hopefully, other women on survival shows or guiding in the mountains and know that girls have adventures too.

I feel passionately that enjoying the wild has nothing to do with your sex. As I've said before, nature doesn't care if you're male or female, it doesn't care what you look like, or what you do for a living, which makes it a really liberating place. Spending time in the wild can free you from convention because it constantly challenges you, giving you the opportunity to find out who you really are and to show yourself – and others – what you're capable of.

The wild doesn't care how old you are either. When I was in my twenties, one of the phrases I heard regularly was 'Oh, I thought you were older.' It can be tempting, especially when you're inexperienced, to want people to like you, but I knew from working with other leaders that if something went wrong, or a tough call had to be made, I had to have enough personal authority that my clients wouldn't question me. I can always explain later why I'm asking them to do something. I took the comments about my age as a sign that I was doing my job well enough for people to think I was older.

When I first started leading, I'm not sure I properly understood how much responsibility I was taking on, especially as you can never know if you're any good at it until you're put under pressure and challenged. There are some people who want to be able to say, 'Oh, I've just led a group out to Afghanistan', or wherever, because they think it's cool: they don't understand the massive responsibility they have until the shit hits the fan and it's down to them to solve a problem.

And it really is a massive burden: on the ground, leaders have sole responsibility for their party and make decisions on their behalf. Often you can't call for help or advice because you're somewhere without a phone signal. You have to have enormous strength in your conviction that you must take a particular course of action. And if it turns out you were wrong, you must have enough belief in yourself to say that at least you stuck by your principles. It's a lot to take on, especially as the industry pays so poorly. Sadly, the low salaries mean many leave the expedition business just as they're coming into their own as leaders.

Some people want to work in the industry because they have a passion for climbing or rafting or diving and see it as a way to make a career of doing something they love, but an affinity for the outdoor life doesn't automatically make you a good leader. In fact, it can do the opposite: your focus is always partly on what you can get out of the trip. I discovered early on that I needed to set aside my own ambitions for an expedition: the client is paying, and that means their experience takes precedence over mine. I get a lot of emails from people who say they want to be an outdoor instructor, but when I talk to them, I realise they just want to be paid for doing their hobby. It's great they've got the passion – that was how I started in the industry – but you also need the temperament to take responsibility for other people's lives.

When I'm recruiting people to work with me, I always look at their qualifications as well as their experience. It's great to have applicants with years of experience, but I want to see that they've taken their career seriously enough to get the basic qualifications. There are plenty of people who think the work I do, especially the TV work, is adrenaline-filled thrill-a-minute stuff, playing with helicopters and seeing the world, but it's serious work, and if I'm going to be putting my life in someone else's hands, I want to know they've covered the basics.

Since that first mountain-leader certificate, I've gone on to get qualifications in swift water rescue, medicine in remote areas, Alpine and Nordic skiing, mountain-biking, off-road driving, industrial rope access and rock-climbing, as well as International Mountain qualifications survival and bushcraft. They don't just give employers confidence in my abilities: they give me confidence, which helps me to be a better leader.

I'm not always in charge. When I'm part of the safety crew on TV shows, I'll sometimes work under someone else, and because the work we do has the potential to get dangerous very quickly, it's really important that you trust the person in charge. Sometimes that person is Stani, which I found hard initially, after we'd got together – it still is occasionally: when we're not at work, we're equals, we both have owner-ship of our lives and make decisions jointly.

Interestingly, he says that when he's working under me, he doesn't find it difficult. I'd love to understand the psychological reasoning why I feel differently. Is it my insecurity as a woman, the desire to be recognised or because I don't want to be submissive to my partner? I honestly don't know, but we go to great lengths to be professional. Which, I guess, is good for our careers, but I wonder if maybe it's not so good for the relationship to be hiding it, to switch off the responses you would normally show your partner.

One aspect of leadership I'm increasingly aware of is the importance of constantly being tested. When the same person is in charge for too long, complacency can set in. As a part-Siberian husky, Tug is a pack animal. I can see that she's constantly testing Stani and me to make sure we're strong enough. In a pack of wolves, the younger animals are always challenging the dominant one. Instead of creating instability, this appears to be an evolutionary process that makes the whole pack stronger. The more you test your leader, the better his or her leadership. You also get cohesion, because everyone in the group – the company or the country – trusts the decisions that are being made on their behalf.

I often think about the wolf pack when I'm working on shows similar to *The Island*. In situations where there isn't an appointed leader, you see contestants vying to be top dog by constantly having a go at each other. Often, you see typical alpha personalities try to dominate the argument, but although that kind of behaviour might mean you end up in charge of the group, it doesn't follow that you're going to be a good leader.

A lot of the men we think of as alpha personalities aren't really. A real alpha personality doesn't need to get into fights and verbal bust-ups to show their dominance because they have natural qualities that mean you respect them. And if you respect someone, you're more likely to follow them. In the adventure business, you meet a lot of people – usually men – who perform the part of an alpha male but lack the in-built qualities of one. Very often good leaders aren't always at the front.

On *The Island*, it's usually the case that by the end of the group's stay, an unexpected leader has emerged, someone who didn't get a lot of attention in the first week. They're often a bit older and a lot calmer, the sort of person you feel safe with. The sort of person you can talk to. And because people have talked to them, they've gained a lot of information about the other contestants, which gives them a certain natural power. We tend to like people who listen to us or make us feel heard, so when the quieter personalities emerge as leaders, you often see a boost in the group's morale.

When you're making TV shows, the performance aspect of alpha behaviour is even more apparent, especially when celebrity egos are involved: it's sometimes very obvious that someone is just trying to get noticed by the producers. But there's no mistaking true leadership when you see it. On the second series of *Mission Survive*, it was interesting that many of the contestants naturally looked to Stuart Pearce for leadership. Stuart, a former footballer and manager, was one of the older men in the group and was physically tall and strong, but he was reluctant to take charge, even when the rest of the group wanted him to.

He was very softly spoken to begin with, and even though he didn't want to be the leader, the other contestants naturally deferred to him. He turned out to be such a natural leader. He was just so aware of how things would come across on camera that he kept taking people to one side and saying, 'If you do this or that, they'll eliminate you.' He made the cohesion in the team. In a survival situation, that's brilliant, but when you're making a TV show you need sparks to fly. Once he was safely back at the hotel, the cohesion within the group started to break down as there wasn't another natural leader to take his position. Almost immediately there were lots more little arguments as different characters emerged.

There are lots of examples – in business and politics, particularly – of things going wrong for a group when a strong leader steps aside. This is why it's important that other people are ready to step up if something happens to the person in charge. My presence can be so reassuring to some clients that they switch off and assume I will take care of everything. That dependency is dangerous, and when I sense people are becoming too reliant on me, I find ways for them to start believing in themselves, or at least taking decisions for themselves. On *Mission Survive*, where it was my role to travel with the participants and keep them safe, some contestants looked to me for approval before they attempted anything. When you're trying to make a TV show, such dependency can alter the narrative so I had to make sure I was out of sight when certain sequences were filmed so the cameras could get the contestants' natural reactions.

A group needs to be able to survive if something happens to its leader, but the leader also needs the group to take action if necessary. If I require emergency medical attention, I need the people I'm with to either give that help or go and get it. A leader who wants only to dominate is potentially doing harm not just to the group but to themselves.

I can be loud and forceful if I need to be, but it's not my natural state. What's important is that, if there's a crisis, I have authority, which means I can't rely on a single leadership style. If I read a client as being hostile towards women, for example, I need to find a way of compensating for that hostility. If I have a group of clients who are scared, then my leadership style will be more nurturing. Good leaders need to be chameleons who can adapt to their group and the situation they find themselves in.

That kind of flexibility is more energy-consuming than being prescriptive on how an expedition should run, but it allows me to get more out of my clients, and them to get much more from the expedition. I try hard not to be the leader who drags people from A to B: I'd much rather give them a map and a compass and show them how they can reach the destination themselves. I want my clients to share my love of the wilderness, and the more I can help them to understand their environment, the more I think I can call myself a good leader.

16

The Selfish Mind

Early in my career I was leading a long trek in Nepal. We were about ten days into the expedition and were going through a pass at just over six thousand metres. The weather was starting to change, so we ended up stuck for a night in a teahouse. There is a network of teahouses – little more than huts, really – run by local families throughout the Himalayas that provide basic shelter and food, but not much else because they're so isolated.

In the teahouse we found a climber – a Belgian guy in his thirties – who must have fallen because he'd broken his arm and the bone was actually sticking out through the flesh. I say 'must have fallen' because I don't know: he was slipping in and out of consciousness and couldn't tell me very much.

The Sherpa accompanying us managed to find out that he had come in with a friend four days previously, but the other man had left that morning. This guy had a broken arm, a horrific infection, because the wound hadn't been treated, and his friend had abandoned him to his fate. I couldn't believe anyone would do that.

The Belgian guy was being looked after by the teahouse owner and his wife. They were doing everything they could, but they had no way of treating the infection. No one had passed through for several days, so there hadn't been anyone who could help with transferring him to a hospital.

I did what I could to disinfect the wound and administered general antibiotics, but he needed expert medical help. That meant getting him to Kathmandu but it was a four-day trek over tough terrain just to get to the nearest road. There was no means of transport available: it was walk or die. But he couldn't go anywhere because he was suffering from severe altitude sickness.

There are different degrees of altitude sickness. Most people will suffer some symptoms above three thousand metres, like headaches or nausea, shortness of breath or trouble sleeping. This guy had acute mountain sickness (AMS), which can deteriorate very quickly into two fatal conditions: high-altitude pulmonary oedema (HAPE), where fluid builds up in your lungs, like drowning, because there's so much pressure in your thoracic cavity; or high-altitude cerebral oedema (HACE), which means there's a lot of fluid in the brain. Pressure starts to build within the skull and you end up 'coning' as the brain is squished by the fluid into the spinal cord.

The company I was working for provided us with Gamow bags, which were developed for temporary use in emergency situations – like bad weather or darkness – where it's not possible to take a patient down to a lower altitude. They are basically long rubber tubes that you put the patient inside. You then inflate them with a foot pump to create a hyper-baric chamber. This allows you to increase the air pressure around the patient; depending on the altitude you're working at, it may have the same effect as carrying them down several thousand metres. It helps stabilise their symptoms. By putting him in the Gamow bag, we were giving him a chance to get well enough to seek help for his wound.

My medical kit included nifedipine and dexamethasone, both of which combat the symptoms of AMS. Diamox can aid in acclimatisation by dilating the capillaries to let the blood flow more quickly. But the single best way to treat AMS is to get the patient down the mountain or, failing that, to put them into a Gamow bag because the increase in pressure allows the body to absorb more oxygen.

We spent most of the night pumping the Gamow bag to keep the pressure up (which can be quite dangerous for those doing the pumping as it increases their risk of succumbing to AMS), and in the morning a couple of my porters took him down. The rest of us carried on with our trek but the nature of mountain travel meant I never saw the porters again and never found out what happened to the Belgian guy. I often think about him. I also think about the 'friend' who abandoned him. At the time, I couldn't understand how anyone could walk away from a friend in such a desperate situation, but over the years I've wondered if maybe, under certain conditions, I might have made the same choice.

I'd always assumed that the two must have been really good mates, but it subsequently occurred to me that perhaps they were just two guys who had met in a hostel in Kathmandu and decided to go on a trek together. Maybe the second man realised how badly injured his friend was and went off in search of medical help. More likely he panicked. He was in a remote place with a dying man and teahouse owners who didn't speak English. No one had passed through since their arrival and he must have been scared. Maybe he was suffering from altitude sickness himself. Maybe he thought he would die up there if he didn't make the journey down while he still could.

In mountaineering circles, there's quite a lot of talk about how human behaviour changes at altitude. Above seven thousand metres, the terrain is known as the 'death zone' because your body is so starved of oxygen you're dying. No one can stay there for long, and it's unbelievably energy-sapping, especially as you only get that high after enduring weeks of climbing. When people fall over at those heights, they sometimes never get up: they are so exhausted. I have heard a lot of stories about other mountaineers walking past the dying and leaving them to their fate. People who aren't mountaineers find this hard to believe, but when you have barely enough energy to save yourself, can you be sure you'd stop to help? Does having the survivor mindset mean you'd put yourself first, even if it meant someone else dying?

I think that, unless you've been in a survival situation, you can't judge the behaviour of those who have had to make such a choice. One of the most famous survival stories is that of the Uruguayan football team who survived a plane crash in the Andes in 1972. It was turned into a movie, *Alive*, and is best known because a few of the survivors, in utter desperation, resorted to eating some of the victims of the crash. Their bodies had been preserved in the snow, and after weeks of not being found, the survivors were close to death themselves. A lot of people say they could never do such a thing, but if you thought you might die, can you be absolutely sure you wouldn't?

There are other stories you hear on the adventure circuit that go beyond cannibalism to murder. Groups get stranded and perhaps two people leave camp to find food but only one person comes back. They seem to have a bit more energy. Do you believe their story that their companion slipped and fell down a cliff, or do you harbour suspicions that they killed to get a meal?

Sadly, there's enough evidence of how quickly society can break down when people think there won't be consequences to their actions. The World Health Organisation has reported increases in violent crime after numerous disasters ranging from volcanic eruptions to hurricanes, and even during the London riots of 2011 we saw a surge in looting. The sad fact is some people will exploit chaos and tragedy for their own gain. Now, imagine you're in a survival situation with some of those people: not only do they think they won't be caught, they think they might die soon.

For some reason, we believe that if we're unfortunate enough to be shipwrecked we'll be stranded with morally upstanding people. We don't seem to consider the possibility that we could be on that desert island with strangers who have a history of violence, or individuals from whom we have very different views; neither do we think about what desperate people might do to survive. I travel a lot in remote places and I'm often the only white woman on the plane: if there's a crash, how would the other survivors treat me? In theory we should have a better chance of survival if we stick together, but it's not hard for me to see there might be situations in which I'd be safer if I went off alone.

For me, because of the work I do, I'm statistically more likely to find myself in a survival scenario because an expedition has gone wrong, rather than because the ship I've been sailing on has sunk, which skews the profile of the people I'm likely to be with in that survival situation. I might be with individuals who have recently been through trauma, which could mean they're suffering from post-traumatic stress disorder. Maybe their PTSD will be triggered by the stress we're dealing with, and who's to say how that will affect their behaviour? If you thought the people you were with posed a threat to your survival, might you wander off into the wilderness alone?

I've been thinking a lot lately about the threat posed by other humans because of the documentary series I've been planning about my solo trip to Alaska. The idea is for me and Tug to walk from the far north to Anchorage. It's a journey I want to take because I really feel the need to test myself. Recently in my expedition and TV work I have to rein things in slightly to keep everyone safe. It's left me with a powerful yearning to test my responses and reflexes properly and explore again my tolerance of risk. The idea is to get as close to the wilderness as possible so I'll be taking the absolute minimum: basic shelter, a rifle, an axe, a knife and a medical pack.

The big risks I'll face will be bears, wolves (and that's more because of Tug than me), moose, exposure, starvation, dehydration, injury, drowning and human error. I'm taking the rifle so I can hunt to eat, but I might also have to use it to kill predators. I've been forced to consider what would happen if I came across a human predator.

You have to question why someone would be alone in a remote wilderness. Are they a loner, a hunter, a fugitive? As humans are pack animals, we're not usually accustomed to living alone, and there's probably a very good reason why someone has shut themselves off from the world. It's not unreasonable to think the isolated homesteader has turned their back on society for a reason, and if they haven't had human contact for months I'm not sure I'd want to be their reintroduction to society!

I was talking to the production crew about the Alaska trip,

and at first we thought it would make really good footage if I interacted with all the ranchers who live along the route. But as a woman travelling alone, I could be putting myself in unnecessary danger. Would I find myself in a situation where I had to shoot first? Could I kill somebody to save myself?

I gave a lot of thought to that, and the answer I came up with was . . . probably. I don't know what the psychological impact would be, but if my life was in danger, I think I'd have to find out.

Increasingly I'm recognising that I'm probably capable of all sorts of things I had previously assumed I wasn't. Writing this book has made me think even more about what it really takes, mentally, to survive, and I keep coming back to this: if I'm leading an expedition and there's a freak accident or something has gone catastrophically wrong, would I ever leave my clients if I thought I couldn't save them? If I could increase my own chances of survival by abandoning them, would I walk away? Could I actually do that? How bad would things have to be before I would consider it?

If I thought by going alone I could reach help and raise the alarm, I'd definitely leave, but if there was no chance of rescue, what then? Could I really do that and save myself? I want to say, 'No, of course not, never,' but I've seen how people's behaviour changes when they're in extreme distress: I'm not sure that any of us can truly know. If I was the only woman in a group of strangers, it's more likely I would disappear. If those men were Stani and Bear, or someone else with their skills, then obviously we'd be better off together. But if we were somewhere where food or water was scarce and there just weren't the resources for all of us to survive, what would I do? What would you do?

If it came to it, it might not even be a conscious decision because – from everything I've learnt over the years – when you're right on the edge, your body demands to survive. There's a cellular compulsion to fight for every last breath, and once you're free of the cultural expectations imposed on us by society, perhaps it would be easier to walk away than we can imagine.

I hope never to find out if that's part of having a survivor's mind. And as long as I keep doing my job to the best of my abilities, hopefully no one who comes into the wild with me will ever find out either.

Acknowledgements

Every adventure I have had, every expedition I have led, every high and every low has shaped me into who I am and into how I view the world. There are too many people to thank but I am grateful for every interaction I have had throughout my life, both the positive and negative. Each one has taught me to be open minded, to stand up for my beliefs and that it is OK to be yourself with your own quirks and imperfections.

I would like to thank my family for their support, I know I have caused my parents Martin and Lynda quite a bit of stress over the years by not having a 'normal' lifestyle but thank you for sticking it out and being unwavering in your advice and emotional support. To my brother and sisters,

Duncan, Pippa and Laura, I am very proud and lucky to have you all behind me. To my partner Stani for your constant support for 'getting me' far better than I 'get' myself most of the time, I don't know how you put up with my wandering, restlessness. To Finn, Famke, Oliver and Emily the mini adventurers in my life, thank you for the adventures we've shared, I look forward to creating many more memories with you.

I'd love to say a huge thank you to Jo Monroe for the hours spent listening to my ramblings and wrangling my thoughts, views and stories into something comprehensible. You are an inspiration, especially as your own resilience was being tested throughout the whole process.

Thank you to my agent Sarah Manning who initially asked me if I'd like to write a book. Without you this would never have come into existence.

And finally thank you to Charlotte Hardman and her team at Coronet who believed in me and this project.